HOMES THAT COOK

BEST-KEPT SECRETS for Buying, Selling, and Creating a Home

Lettiann Southerland

INDIE BOOKS
INTERNATIONAL

ISBN: 1-941870-20-1
ISBN 13: 978-1-941870-20-4
Library of Congress Control Number: 2015936214

Designed by Joni McPherson, mcphersongraphics.com

INDIE BOOKS INTERNATIONAL, LLC
2424 VISTA WAY, SUITE 316
OCEANSIDE, CA 92054
www.indiebooksintl.com

To my husband Jack:

Thank you for the loving support that you give to me for all of my endeavors.

Here's to the next fifty years of us "cooking" together.

Courtney ‑
So nice meeting you!
Welcome to the OP Chamber.
Happy Cooking!
Jettann
H

TABLE OF CONTENTS

SECTION ONE

What is a Home that Cooks?

What a Home that Cooks Means to Me

Better is a dish of vegetables where love is than a fattened ox served with hatred.

Proverbs 15:17, New American Standard edition

For as long as I can remember, I've always loved to sell stuff. As a child I would set up a table in our front yard and sell candy to the neighborhood kids.

Back then there were candy stores, and their inventory was exclusively candy—all different types and varieties of candy. My mom would take me to the candy store once a week and I'd load up on goods, mark up the price and sell it to the neighborhood kids who never got to go to the candy store. That worked so well that I started selling knickknacks from our house and peddling the items to these same kids, especially around the holidays.

"You gotta get your mom a gift—it's almost Mother's Day," I'd tell them. Yes, they bought. That all ended when my mom found out I was selling her knickknacks to the other kids. My intentions were good and I really enjoyed marketing (trying to get these kids to buy) the goods. I wonder what ever happened to Wacky Wafers. That was the most popular candy that I sold. Every time I see the newer candy Fun Dip I'm reminded of those days. I was destined to be in sales, even back then.

After moving to Kansas City in 1992, I decided to get my real estate license. Prior to that back in Pittsburgh I had worked as a tour operator for USAir, selling group ski trips to the western US ski destinations. What fun I had for those seven years. But I found out that most people drive to the Rockies from Kansas City, so the group ski trip marketing was now over for me.

After the birth of my son, I relinquished my real estate license in order to be a fulltime mom. Now, back in the business, I've been a realtor for more than seven years, and I am enjoying (almost) every minute of it–never a dull moment and no two deals are ever the same.

> My intentions were good and I really enjoyed marketing (trying to get these kids to buy) the goods.

I take pride in knowing that sellers and buyers trust me with the sale and purchase of one of their largest assets.

The Loving Power of a Cookbook

When I first arrived in Kansas City, I was desperately homesick. Leaving my home and family in Pennsylvania was a little more difficult on my heart than I believed it would be. I missed the family dinners, the wine and appetizers under the grape arbor, the laughter and the closeness of my family.

As the youngest of three siblings, I was the last to move out of the state. My oldest brother David moved to New York City after graduating from Auburn University. Eric, the middle sibling, remained in the Chicago area after graduating from Northwestern University. Both brothers are married and I am blessed to have not only them, but two wonderful sisters-in-law, nieces and a nephew.

We were raised in an Italian family in western Pennsylvania where we shared most Sunday meals together at my grandmother's house. My grandfather came to the United States from Lendinara in northern Italy in 1909. In 1914 he met and married my grandmother, also a full-blooded northern Italian, in the town of Meadowlands, Pennsylvania. That same year my grandmother's parents, Peter and Letitia, built a three-story farmhouse in this same town with the intention that the whole family would live there together. My grandmother and grandfather, Baptist and Louise, would occupy the right side of this three-story home and my grandmother's parents, along with her four brothers and one sister occupied the left side of the home. The home shared a center staircase; however, each side had its own living room, dining room, fireplace and full kitchen.

My dad was born in this home in 1928. He would tell my brothers and me about the times when he was growing up there—when, if he didn't like what his mom was cooking for dinner, he'd go over to his Aunt Mary's side of the house to see what she was preparing for dinner. When my great-grandparents built this home in 1914, little did they know it would become a place where generations of happy memories would be made, many of which would include the food that was prepared there and shared there throughout the years—food made with loving hands and generous hearts.

How could I turn my homesickness memories into something that could last a lifetime? My brothers and I grew up learning about food, appreciating food and that dinner was more of an event than just another meal. As I was thinking about the good food and memories, it hit me that I needed to collect all of those recipes from my grandparents, aunts, uncles and cousins before it was too late. I would collect them and then share them with my brothers' families so that they can keep that piece of history and perhaps share the food and memories with their children.

> When my great-grandparents built this home in 1914, little did they know it would become a place where generations of happy memories would be made, many of which would include the food that was prepared there.

As my gift to you, I have shared some of those recipes, along with recipes from other families, with you here in this book. What foods do you most remember or remind you of your family? Are there recipes out there that you would like to pass down or have passed down to you?

More About Meadowlands, Pennsylvania

The entire back yard of this home was a well-maintained garden full of all kinds of food such as Swiss chard, corn, garlic, lettuce, beets, tomatoes, onions—you name it. There was also a cherry tree, two apple trees and one plum tree. Back then it was truly "farm to table".

There was a small area of grass where we often played badminton. I loved hearing my grandmother and my Great Aunt Mary tell me about the outdoor oven that was in the yard back in the day, where they baked bread and other goodies. It sounded like so much fun to me, but I'm certain it was a lot of work for them.

My Aunt Mary and grandmother baked bread weekly until they were in their mid-seventies. Every Wednesday, as I recall, was bread baking day, an all-day event that included kneading, proofing, baking and cooling. They would then wrap each loaf in white freezer paper and tie it with butcher string. I loved Wednesdays.

As you might have guessed, I learned to cook and loved it. My family taught me that preparing food meant so much more than being just "one more thing to do". As I witnessed and learned, sitting down with family and friends to a meal prepared with loving hands and a generous heart not only creates memories but also provides the opportunity for conversation, sharing and strengthening bonds.

Present Day

I am a newlywed of two years, and I have one son and five lovely stepchildren. It brings me such joy to cook for them and introduce them to new foods. Before I met my husband he was a "meat and potatoes" guy and, I've learned, typically kept his food choices quite simple. Well, after two years of marriage that has changed drastically. It is fun now to see my husband sipping fine wine and helping me in the kitchen.

My heart is so happy when I hear my youngest stepson, now sixteen, ask me to make a certain one of my dishes. You have to understand he is the pickiest eater in the family. I'm so delighted that he and the rest of the family are branching out with their food choices. It has been a really fun food journey.

With numerous holidays now under my belt with my husband's side of the family, I've learned that they, too, have some long-standing food traditions. Those recipes can be found in this book as well, as we wanted to preserve them for our kids.

What recipes, foods and traditions do you enjoy with your family? Remember to ask family members for those recipes. You'll find pages in this book where you can write some of them down and preserve them for generations to come.

> What recipes, foods and traditions do you enjoy with your family?

And, so, I have taken these two very happy areas of my life and combined them in this book of real estate buying and selling tips along with delicious family recipes, with the hope that they will enrich your life in your quest for a home that cooks.

Enjoy.

Lettiann Southerland

March 2015

SECTION TWO

Buying a Home that Cooks

Tips for Buying a Home

1. **Before house hunting, get pre-approved.** Getting pre-approved makes it clear what you can afford so you will not waste time looking at houses that are out of your price range. In addition, when you do find the right house you will be in a better position to make a serious offer.

2. **Start by looking at your credit.** Most people need to apply for mortgages to buy a home, so take the time now to look through your credit history and be sure it is accurate and clean.

3. **Aim for a home you can really afford.** Don't set yourself up for disappointment or financial grief. There are many online calculators to help you understand how your income, debts, and expenses affect what you can afford.

4. **Buy in a district with good schools.** This may not seem important if you don't have children, but it is often a top priority for home buyers. Therefore, even if you will never have a need for those good schools, when it comes time to sell, it will boost your property values.

5. **Get professional help.** An exclusive buyer agent will be looking out for your best interests and can help you navigate the bidding and buying process. The best part is, since the seller of the home pays the buyer's agent, you will pay very little and they can probably save you a substantial amount of money.

6. **Do your homework before bidding.** Look at comparable homes in your neighborhood that have sold in the past three months. Your opening bid should be based on these trends.

7. **Hire a home inspector.** Don't rely on the seller's information— hire your own certified home inspector who will evaluate the home on your behalf and make you aware of potential problems that could be expensive to fix later.

8. **Keep your money where it is.** Remember this is a huge financial transaction and your finances are being examined. Avoid possible red flags by refraining from major purchases and significant money transfers for three to six months before buying a new home.

9. **Don't obsess with trying to time the market.** There is no perfect time to buy and you'll make yourself crazy trying to predict the housing market. The best time is when you have found the right house for you at a price you can afford.

10. **Bigger isn't always better.** It may seem like opting for the best and biggest house would make sense but it is actually the opposite. You have to remember that the largest house in the neighborhood is not going to appeal to many potential buyers when it comes time to sell the house in the future.

11. **Stalk the neighborhood.** Some neighborhoods are very different by day, or by night. To avoid being surprised after the fact, visit the area at various hours to see what's going on.

12. **Think long-term and think resale.** While we are talking about *buying* a house, not *selling*, it is important to consider your plans for the next few years and whether the house will be easy to sell in the future when you are ready to move on.

13. **Make a checklist of your must-haves, nice-to-haves, and other essentials.** This may seem obvious but emotional reactions to houses can be strong and make you forget the realities. Have a list in writing so you can check the house against it—if it doesn't have your must-haves, do you really love it?

14. **Look at *all* the expenses when you are budgeting for the house.** If you are only budgeting for the principal, interest, taxes, and insurance, you may be surprised in the long-run. Think about other factors like upgrades you'll need to make to the house and changes in costs of utilities and commuting that will affect your bottom line.

15. **Ask for the homeowners association covenants before you make a decision.** If your house is part of a HOA, you have

to abide by all their rules—so make sure you read them first. You may find that certain conditions do not fit your needs; for example, preventing you from making improvements or renting the house.

16. **Read your contract before you sign it.** This should be a given, but it bears saying that you must fully read and understand your contract. Since this is probably the biggest purchase of your life, if you have questions about anything in the document, ask your mortgage broker and your real estate agent.

17. **Look beyond the staging (or lack thereof).** As you look at houses, try to ignore the staging and pay attention to the layout and structure of the house. Ugly paint colors or décor can distract some buyers but those are easy fixes. On the other hand, beautiful staging often disguises problems you may have seen in an empty house. Try to mentally clear out the space and go from there.

18. **Explore mortgage options.** Mortgages are not one-size-fits-all—different banks offer different interest rates and terms. Consider your plans for the future and shop around to determine what best fits your goals.

19. **Understand the offer process.** Don't make a blind guess. I already mentioned you should know the price of comparable properties that sold in the neighborhood, but you should also know how that compares to currently available properties. Even knowing how long the house has been on the market can help you decide what to offer. Also, know that you will most likely need to negotiate, so don't offer the most you can afford on your first go.

20. **Be prepared for competition when making an offer.** If this house is perfect, you are probably not the only one who thinks so. You may be up against others who are after the same house so make a good offer and discuss with your agent ways to distinguish yourself from the crowd of buyers.

21. **Find the right neighborhood.** The house is important but the neighborhood is just as crucial to your happiness. It isn't just about commute times. Think about what is important in your daily

life that you want in this new home base. Do you like outdoor recreation spaces? Do you need nearby nightlife and restaurants? Are you concerned with good schools and safe spaces for children?

22. **Don't allow yourself to be pressured by the seller or the real estate agent.** This is a major decision—don't allow yourself to be rushed. If you are unsure, ask people you trust for help and advice and take the time you need to be clear you are making the right choice.

SECTION THREE

Selling a Home that Cooks

Tips for Selling a Home

1. **Don't attend your open house.** Think back to when you were shopping for a house—would you have felt comfortable to speak your mind with the owner hovering? Give serious buyers room to have an honest conversation with each other and their agent without feeling the need to edit themselves.

2. **Don't pretend to be a buyer at your open house.** This will likely backfire and you will drive away real potential buyers with this crazy behavior. If you feel like you need feedback, ask your agent to tell you the useful comments from the open house.

3. **Provide attractions not distractions.** You want to showcase your home and appeal to buyers, but go too far and you could detract. There is nothing wrong with providing cool drinks on a hot day to make buyers more comfortable—it could motivate them to stay longer and see more of the house. Offering a full meal, however, would be unnecessary and distracting.

4. **Consider seasonal preferences.** While preparing your property and taking steps to market it to potential buyers, consider what seasonal aspects will be appealing while you are selling it. A roaring fire in winter or beautiful spring blooms may help you get a better offer. This may seem silly, but research has shown that buyers are willing to pay more for houses with swimming pools in the summer than in the winter.

5. **Provide full access to the property.** You want to be sure buyers can view your whole property when they visit. Unless there is a safety issue, you should not make any rooms, closets, or areas off limits. It is called an open house, after all.

6. **Hold your open house during common times.** If at all possible, schedule your open house at the same time as others in

the area. Potential buyers often spend a few hours on Sundays and want to maximize their time and see multiple properties while they are out. Though it may be more convenient for you to do it another time, you may limit the number of people that can attend.

7. **Don't neglect the neighbors.** Your neighbors are good assets—they may know people who want to live in the neighborhood and can tell their friends about your property. Invite them to your open houses and offer flyers they can pass along.

8. **Price it right.** How do you know what to set for the price? Have it evaluated by an appraiser for its value, then lower that number by 15 to 20 percent. This may sound counterintuitive, but this will likely cause a bidding war between potential buyers that may drive the price up even higher than it's worth.

9. **Make sure your closets are half-empty.** You know that buyers like to look in every door, so you must always keep closets and cabinets clean and organized. But a great tip is to take half of your things out of the closets and make what is left extremely neat. All buyers are looking for lots of storage space and this trick makes all your closets appear larger.

10. **Maximize the light in your home.** A bright and cheery house is more sellable. Do whatever you can to increase the light, including removing drapes, cleaning windows, and changing to higher-wattage light bulbs.

11. **Play the agent field.** You need the best broker for the job—don't feel like you are stuck if it isn't working out. Your broker should have a good grasp of technology with access to all the best tools and be very well informed about other properties in your neighborhood.

12. **Conceal your pets.** Evidence of pets can be a huge turnoff for buyers because it gives the impression that the house is not clean (especially if they smell the litter box or wet-dog odors). During open houses, send pets to a family member's house or a kennel for the day.

13. **Don't over-upgrade.** Though it may seem like it will help, major home improvements right before selling your house usually do not pay off. Don't spend a nickel unless you can turn it into a dime. Small updates will be far more worthwhile: painting the walls, changing out door handles and cabinet hardware, fixing leaky faucets, and cleaning tile grout.

14. **Take the home out of your house.** You probably love how "homey" your house is, but when selling the house you want a clean slate for buyers to picture themselves in. Remove one-third of your belongings and put them in storage—especially family photos and personal keepsakes that don't have a broad appeal. If you are unsure of what to do, there are professional home stagers that will help you to show off your home in the best light.

15. **Improve the kitchen.** One area where upgrades usually see a return is the kitchen. Even something as simple as painting the walls and cabinets and upgrading the hardware can have a major impact. If you are able to invest a little more, buy one high-end stainless steel appliance.

16. **Always be ready to show.** This can be difficult, but your house needs to be in perfect condition so as many prospective buyers as possible can come by at any time. If you aren't available or if your timing is very restrictive you may alienate people who don't want to deal with the hassle.

17. **Stage the exterior of your home, too.** Staging the house is not just about the inside—the exterior needs attention as well. Your landscaping and paint job should be in great shape. You may want to invest in furniture for your backyard so that buyers can picture themselves using that space.

18. **Audit your agent's online marketing.** Have you seen your online listing? Research reveals 92 percent of homebuyers start their house hunt online. Do you have an enticing listing and pictures that attract buyers?

19. Let your neighbors choose their neighbors. Check into neighborhood message boards or newsletters to see if you can send the listing out to neighbors. As I mentioned before, inviting neighbors to open houses can help sell the area to potential buyers.

20. Facebook your home's listing. Your social network is a good resource. Reach to your connections on Facebook to spread the word about your house being on the market.

21. Beat the competition with condition. If your neighborhood has very low-priced foreclosures, you will not be able to compete on price. But most of those properties will be in very poor condition. Appeal to the buyers looking for quality by looking at details like broken knobs and handles, scratches, or other things that need repairs and taking care of those before you start showing the house.

22. Get clued into your competition. It is good to know what you are up against. Research comparable houses for sale in your area. Attend open houses and notice what stands out to you—both negatives and positive—since similar things will be seen by buyers at your house. Make sure that the condition of your house stacks up to others that your potential buyers will be looking at.

23. De-clutter. Your surfaces should be as clear as possible, so pack up or sell all your knickknacks or other items sitting on top of counters, tables or other flat surfaces. If you need to, put things into storage.

24. Listen to your agent. Spend time finding the right agent, one that you can trust, with a lot of experience. Then listen and follow the advice your agent is giving to you.

25. Sweeten the deal. In a down market, you can distinguish yourself by offering a deal to buyers. Some sellers offer money toward closing costs, or even pay them entirely.

26. Move fast. Some buyers want to close very quickly, especially if they have been searching for a house for a long time. If you are able to close on the house within thirty to sixty days, you may get their attention.

27. **Get your home in "move-in" condition.** To speed up the process and make your house more appealing, take care of any necessary fixes to doors, appliances, or plumbing that isn't in compliance.

28. **Do pre-inspection repairs.** Along those same lines, you probably know some of the issues the inspector will discover. Get ahead of the game and fix it now before the buyer needs to ask you to do so.

29. **Pressure-wash the driveway and any decks.** You never get a second chance at a first impression, so make sure your property impresses the moment they get out of the car. A clean driveway and deck will reflect the quality of the house inside.

30. **Clean the windows.** This is often overlooked, but will make a big difference in terms of light and a pleasant view outside. Be sure to wash them inside and out.

31. **Leave neutral furniture and accessories.** As I mentioned before, you want to get rid of personal items and photos, but don't go too far and get rid of everything. Neutral furniture and accessories will actually help the buyer picture themselves in the house better than a completely empty house.

32. **Clean and redo the laundry room.** Don't forget about the laundry room—it is often overlooked in daily life but it is worth sprucing up while selling a house. Keep the colors light and maybe repaint and replace baskets and towels.

33. **Organize pots and pans.** The same rule of closets applies to the kitchen—clear it out. Pack up the extra, rarely used kitchen items and your cabinets will look much larger.

34. **Always follow the "clean clean clean" rule.** Cleanliness is next to godliness, they say—and this is especially true in the eyes of buyers. When you are selling a house, you should clean thoroughly, paying attention to tiny details like light switches, door knobs, and anything that is touched often. If you can't do a good enough job, hire a professional.

35. Have a complete information sheet about the house.
Though this should be provided by your realtor, you should check that it is accurate and mentions key things. Be on top of having enough copies to give to every potential buyer.

36. Do your own assessment. It is easy to become accustomed to your surroundings so that you no longer really see them. Try to shift your perspective to see things as buyers will. Stand in front of your house—what stands out? Is there anything you notice as you walk in the front door? Even better, get some fresh eyes: ask friends to come by assess it for you.

37. Place fresh flowers on tables. Flowers can brighten the whole room. Include them on tables throughout the house for open houses.

38. Appeal to the woman first. Women tend to make the final decision about whether to buy, or not buy, a home. Even single men usually consider whether they would bring a date over. If you are a single man, you might want to ask the women in your life to look at the house to be sure it appeals to female buyers.

39. Go for "wow moments." Each room in the house should include a "wow moment"—something that is unexpected. Let the buyers discover these "wow moments" for themselves as they go through the house.

40. Keep a good mindset. Don't be discouraged—maintain a positive attitude and try not to take things personally. There are buyers out there that want your exact property—just be patient and you will find them.

Home Staging and Organization

Tips for a quick sale with the benefits of home staging

Buyers are looking for "that feel." They want to walk into a house and have it feel warm and inviting. Effective use of space, furnishings, paint and accessories can do wonders in this area.

You don't want to make the buyer ask, "I wonder what kind of people live in this home?"

You want buyers to say, "I can see myself living here."

The rooms in your house that matter the most are the kitchen, living room, master bedroom, and master bathroom. You really want to impress potential buyers with these spaces. Focus on updating, de-personalizing, de-cluttering, and neutralizing these spaces.

When a home is staged, it sells quicker, for a better price, and with fewer negotiations. If you take the time to do home repairs, and spend some money up front for staging and upgrades, it will pay off in the end. Don't give the buyer a reason to offer a lower price on your house.

Disassociate yourself with your home

- Say to yourself, "This is not my home; it is a house—a product to be sold."
- The way you live in your home, and the way that your home is marketed and sold, are two very different things.
- Make a mental decision to let go of your emotions and focus on the fact that soon this house will no longer be yours.

- Say goodbye to every room.
- Don't look back—look forward to the future.

Depersonalize and De-Clutter

- Pack up personal photographs and family heirlooms. Buyers can't see past personal artifacts and you don't want them to be distracted.

- People collect an amazing quantity of junk. If you don't need it, donate it or throw it away.

- A big part of staging is just packing up early. Pack away things you can live without for a while. Make sure closets and cabinets aren't overcrowded.

- Pack away knickknacks and collectibles. It is distracting to buyers. We want them to stay focused on the house.

- Clean off kitchen counters. Find a home for your toaster, coffee maker, mixer, etc. in a cabinet or pantry.

- In the bathroom, put toiletry and shower items out of sight and into a container that can be stored under the sink.

- Storage areas and garages need to be addressed as well. These spaces need to be organized and de-cluttered.

Streamline Closets and Cabinets

- Buyers love to snoop and will open closet and cabinet doors. Think of the message it sends if things are messy and disorganized. Now imagine what a buyer believes about you if they see everything organized and neatly in its place. It says you probably take good care of the rest of your home as well. Fabric bins, woven baskets, and plastic storage containers give a wonderful organized and streamlined look.

- A few ideas to get you started: Neatly stack dishes, turn coffee cup handles facing the same way, hang shirts together, buttoned and facing the same way on white hangers, line up your shoes, straighten and color coordinate stacks of towels in the linen closet, organize food by size and type in the pantry.

Rent a Storage Unit or POD

- Almost every home shows better with less furniture.
- Give each room a single purpose. You don't want the buyer wondering "Now what is this room used for?"

Make Minor Repairs

- Patch holes in walls.
- Touch up paint on walls and trim.
- Fix leaky faucets.
- Fix doors that don't close properly and kitchen drawers that jam.
- Replace burned out light bulbs.
- Repaint walls in warm neutral colors. (You don't want buyers to remember your home as "that house with the orange bathroom")
- If you have considered replacing worn bedding—Do so now. Especially in the master. The master needs to have the feel of a luxury hotel room.
- Less is more when it comes to window coverings. Remove heavy draperies. Open blinds and let the light shine in.

Make the House Sparkle

- Clean. Clean. Clean.
- Wipe down baseboards, trim, and switch plates.
- Wash windows inside and out.
- Clean out cobwebs high and low.

These staging tips courtesy of:

Amy Scheuerman with Creative Solutions Home Staging and Organization, Kansas City, Missouri. E-mail: creativesolutionsKC@gmail.com

Seller Maintenance Checklist

Step back and take some quality time to look at your home through the eyes of a buyer. Here is a checklist of items you should address before putting the "For Sale" sign in the front yard:

1. **Paint.** A fresh coat of paint on the interior walls can really do wonders. Stay neutral throughout.

2. **Curb appeal.** How do you look from the street? Pick up leaves, prune lower branches from trees, clean out flower beds and add a touch of color splash to the front, such as an urn with flowers or garden bench with colorful pillows.

3. **Driveway and sidewalks.** Are they in need of repair? Are there major cracks and elevation changes? If so, contact a professional as major cracks in these areas can hinder a sale for safety reasons.

4. **Roof. Be honest.** If you are in need of a new roof, it's best to replace it now or price your home accordingly.

5. **Appliances.** How are they operating and are any of the major appliances, including the HVAC in need of repair? Keep service records so buyers can sense the items in the home were well-maintained.

6. **Pick up and purge.** Now is a good time to remove the excess items in your home.

7. **Wood rot.** Inspect the exterior window and door frames and the interior windows for wood rot. Make a list and have a quality handyperson repair and repaint before you open your doors to would-be buyers.

7. **Carpets.** Have all wall-to-wall carpets cleaned. Clean carpets make a really good first impression. If they are in too bad shape to clean, replace them. If you have carpeting in the bathroom, it's best to remove it and replace it with flooring other than carpet.

8. **Lights.** Make sure all fixtures, including ceiling fans and ceiling fixtures, have working light bulbs.

9. **Smell.** Does the interior of your home smell pleasant? If you're not sure, ask neighbors to walk through your home and tell you what they smell. If pet odors are prevalent please know that that is a big buyer turn off. Smelly plug-ins and sprays often create an even worse combination of smells. Perhaps the new carpet and new paint will help with pet and smoke odors. Keep litter boxes well off the beaten path of buyers. Keep Fido contained during showings, as well.

11. **Smoke detectors.** Are they all in working order?

12. **Home warranty.** Consider purchasing a home warranty.

13. **Home inspection.** Consider having your home pre-inspected by a qualified licensed home inspector.

Seller Realtor Interview Questions

1. How familiar are you with the area in which I live?

2. What do you know about the school district where my house is located?

3. Have you sold anything in this area or surrounding areas?

4. Do you work full time selling real estate or do you work part time?

5. What is your list-price-to-sales-price ratio?

6. What data can you show me that would support the right price market value for my home?

7. Are you a good negotiator?

8. What type of marketing plan will you implement for my home?

9. Who am I going to be dealing with throughout my transaction?

10. How often will I hear from you and by what method? Phone, e-mail or text?

11. What is your business philosophy?

12. How do you handle showings and showing requests?

13. Please provide contact information for three of your most recent clients.

14. Do you have a website and will my home be featured on your site?

15. What separates you from your competition?

Seller Pricing Myths

1. **I'm going to start with a higher list price and see what happens.** If you do this you will likely slow the sale of your home as the buyers who are looking for homes in the price range that your home should be in, will have already purchased a home by the time you drop your price. Price your house right the first time, based on the current market data that your real estate agent will provide.

2. **Minor repairs can wait until later.** Provide a good product (home) from the start. Make all repairs before you go on the market. If you can't afford to do so, be sure to price the home accordingly.

3. **Tell buyers to make an offer, any offer.** Buyers aren't out looking for more house than they can afford or more than their lender approved them for. So, likely the buyers that can afford your home for the price that it is actually worth, won't be looking at it at all.

4. **I'm going to sell my house on my own to avoid paying commission.** You go to a dentist when you have a tooth concern, right? Why wouldn't you hire a professional to sell one of your largest assets? Paying for the professional services of a real estate agent in the end pays off for the seller. He or she provides objectivity without the emotional factor. Here's why:

    *   The knowledge and experience that a real estate agent brings to the table certainly will outweigh the cost if you hire a realtor with the right fit. What about litigation? Writing the contract and addendums? Did the seller (you) disclose all material facts, defects and repairs?

    *   Do you want people calling you and ringing your doorbell at any hour of the day or night?

- Exposure. The number of people a real estate agent can reach will likely exceed what a FSBO can do. Do you have a relocation department in your basement, for example?

5. **The real estate agent will set the price for my home.** No. But he or she will (should) provide you with all the most recent market data that would support the right price for your home.

SECTION FOUR

Creating a Home that Cooks Recipes

Favorites from Lettiann's Kitchen

Two Cents' Worth: Kitchen Tidbits

1. Have separate cutting boards for different foods, i.e., one specifically for raw meats, one for vegetables and garlic, one for fruits and one for cheeses. Cutting all of the same foods on the same board can not only be a health hazard, but foods can pick up the smell of previous foods that were cut, even after the boards have been washed.

2. Different colored cutting boards can help you tell them apart: red for raw meats/poultry, green for vegetables and garlic, white for fruit. Perhaps a nice wood board or marble slab for cheese cutting and serving.

3. Salt your pasta water as soon as you fill up the pot. Bring water to a rolling boil and add pasta. Never add oil to pasta water. You don't want sticky pasta. Be sure to cook it al dente and rinse in cold water, unless you are adding the pasta directly from the boiling water to your sauce. Cooked pasta should be firm to the touch and have a somewhat chewy texture. If it's soft and mushy, don't serve it.

4. Scented candles are wonderful. However, candle scents do interfere with one's palate and do not belong on the dinner table.

5. Add salt to your water when making hardboiled eggs. It helps to keep the shells from cracking while they are cooking.

6. Unlike cilantro stems, parsley stems should be removed as much as possible before chopping and adding to dishes.

7. Oil and water don't mix. Be sure to dry lettuce leaves and other items you add to your salad before you add the dressing.

8. Use parchment paper as a liner on the sheet pan when baking cookies, bacon or meatballs in the oven. It makes clean up much easier.

9. Remember food odors absorb into other foods that are in the same refrigerator space. You may want to take out pungent foods before you start a dish, or perhaps use a separate refrigerator.

10. When you put hot food into storage containers, be sure to use shallow containers. Foods will cool faster this way before you put them into the freezer. Keep lids off until you are ready to put containers into freezer.

11. If you are sautéing garlic and it burns, throw it out and start over. Burned garlic has an unpleasant taste and odor. It will ruin the taste of your dish.

12. Same with butter—it can turn brown very quickly. If you burn it, throw it out and start over. Combining the butter with a small amount of oil can help keep it from burning so quickly.

13. Use fresh garlic. You may be saving time by purchasing chopped/minced preserved garlic in a jar, but you are definitely sacrificing taste.

14. Always drain and rinse canned beans.

APPETIZERS

Garlicky Eggplant Spread

After a weekend at the lake with girlfriends they suggested giving this dish a different name so their husbands would try it and not be afraid of the "eggplant" word. We came up with the name "Summer Caviar."

2 large eggplants (about 2½ pounds)

2 large cloves garlic, slivered

¼ cup olive oil

2 Tbsp. fresh lemon juice

2 Tbsp. fresh oregano, chopped (or 2 tsp. dried)

1 tsp. ground cumin

Salt and pepper

Red leaf lettuce

4 tomato slices

6 loaves pita bread (7- or 8-inch size)

Preheat oven to 450°. Cut slits in eggplants with tip of knife and insert garlic sliver into each slit. Place eggplants in baking pan and bake until very tender, about 1 hour. Cut each eggplant in half and cool slightly. Scrape eggplant pulp from skin into colander and let drain. Transfer pulp to processor. Add oil, lemon juice, oregano and cumin. Puree until smooth. Season with salt and pepper. Cool completely. Cover and refrigerate. Can be made one day ahead.

PITA CRISPS:

6 loaves pita bread

3 Tbsp. olive oil

Preheat oven to 450°. Brush each pita loaf with olive oil. Cut each loaf into 8 triangles. Arrange pita triangles in a single layer on a large baking sheet. Bake until crisp and golden, about 7 minutes per side.

When ready to serve, line platter with lettuce. Halve, slice, or dice tomatoes and arrange around edge of platter. Mound eggplant mixture in center of platter. Arrange pita crisps around eggplant or serve separately in a basket.

Makes 8 servings.

Donna's Stuffed Sourdough Sandwich

Delicious sandwich with such beautiful presentation. This sandwich looks great displayed on a glass pedestal cake plate when serving.

1 large loaf round bread

3 red bell peppers, cleaned and cut into strips

½ pound fresh spinach, washed and dried

12 thin slices red onion

12 slices salami

12 slices provolone cheese

12 slices turkey breast

Olive oil

Balsamic vinegar

Salt and pepper

Sauté red bell pepper strips in 1 tablespoon olive oil. Cut top off round loaf and hollow out the center. (Reserve insides for another use or feed it to the birds.) Whisk 4 tablespoons olive oil with 2 tablespoons balsamic vinegar; brush mixture inside cavity of bread.

Layer salami, red peppers, spinach, onion, cheese and turkey. Put top back on loaf. Cover entire loaf of bread in plastic, then in foil and refrigerate until flavors blend (4 to 12 hours).

Serve loaf by cutting into wedges like a cake.

Serves 6 to 8.

Salsa Fresca

Pico de Gallo. Great way to use up those summer tomatoes. Great with tortilla chips or use as a topping on eggs and omelets. Add a kick to anything with this fresh salsa.

4 to 5 fresh tomatoes, seeded and diced

2 jalapeños, diced*

1 medium white onion, diced

1 lime

¼ cup fresh cilantro, chopped

Salt

In order to make a nice presentation, dice the tomatoes, jalapeños and onion all the same size. A nice small dice, not minced. Place them into a glass bowl. Squeeze the juice of one lime over the mixture. Add the chopped cilantro, then sprinkle with a generous pinch of salt. Gently stir all ingredients together.

This salsa keeps nicely in the refrigerator for about 3 to 4 days.

Makes almost 2 cups. Recipe can be easily halved.

When chopping the jalapeños, use the seeds to keep the salsa hot, as most of the heat is in the seeds. You may discard the seeds for a milder salsa.

Stuffed Grape Leaves

There are many different fillings for stuffing grape leaves. This recipe is from John Rabler, once a pitcher for our softball team. He would bring a pot filled with these stuffed grape leaves, still steaming hot from his stove, to our games. His version includes fennel seeds, which I found very interesting.

1½ pounds ground chuck

4 strips bacon, chopped pea size

¾ cup long grain rice

Juice of 2 lemons, and a few slices of lemon

3 Tbsp. fennel seeds

Salt and pepper to taste

1 jar grape leaves (or about 30 to 40 if using fresh)

Pick leaves so there is only a small length of stem. Simmer fresh leaves in enough water to cover the leaves for 45 to 60 minutes. If you are unable to pick your own grape leaves, they are available at most grocery stores, and there you will find them packed in brine.

Drain and cool grape leaves. Sauté chopped bacon quickly in a small pan; let cool. Combine ground chuck, cooked bacon, and rice, the juice of 1 lemon, fennel seed, salt and pepper. Lay out a few grape leaves at a time. Fill leaves with meat mixture, according to size of leaf. Fold leaves into bundles. Place all rolled-up bundles into a medium-size stock pot. Layer one on top of the other snugly until all of the bundles are in the pot. Add about 2 cups of water and the juice of the second lemon. Place the slices of lemon on top of the bundle pile. Cover with lid and simmer for 30 to 40 minutes.

NOTE: When purchasing the brine-soaked grape leaves I prefer to drop them gently into boiling water for a minute or two before filling them to get rid of the brine, as it makes the grape leaves have a bitter taste. Fresh grape leaves are best if you are lucky enough to have grapes in your yard. Plant some next spring.

Jan's Cheese Fondue

Best friends, a glass of wine and a warm fire—the recipe for a great evening.

1 pound block white American cheese, shredded

2 cups sour cream

1 tsp. Worcestershire sauce

2 or 3 dashes garlic powder

A hearty loaf of bread, such as French, Italian or sourdough

Apple slices

Heat sour cream. When it's bubbling, drop in shredded cheese a handful at a time. Stir continuously. Add remaining ingredients. When all lumps are smooth, it's done.

Enjoy this fondue with apple slices and large cubes of the bread.

Serves 8 to 10.

Roasted Red Pepper Pesto

Serving suggestions: Use as a dipping sauce for deep fried ravioli—makes a great appetizer. Or toss pesto with hot pasta. Use your imagination for uses for this yummy pesto.

3 roasted red peppers*

½ cup walnuts

⅓ cup olive oil

½ cup fresh grated parmesan cheese

2 Tbsp. fresh basil, rough chopped

2 cloves garlic

Place all ingredients into a food processor. Process until blended thoroughly.

Makes about ½ to ¾ cup.

*Roast peppers over an open flame or under the broiler. Turn peppers often so most of the skin is blackened. When peppers are mostly blackened, place into a paper sack. Fold up the bag so the steam stays inside. When peppers cool remove from sack and peel off all of the charred skin. Remove internal seeds and the stems. Peppers are now ready for your recipe.

Just Punch

Good, quick, cold punch for a party. The ice ring in the punch bowl makes a lovely presentation.

1 to 2 liters 7-Up, cold

½ gallon rainbow sherbet

1 to 2 gallons Hawaiian Punch Fruit Juicy Red

Ice mold

Pour liquid into a punch bowl, as much or as little as it will hold. With an ice cream scoop make balls of rainbow sherbet and put them into the soda mixture in the bowl. Serve immediately.

ICE MOLD: Take a bundt pan and fill with water. Place in freezer until frozen. When you are ready to serve the punch, pop out the ice ring from the pan and place in the punch bowl. It will float, and is a lovely presentation when you place the balls of sherbet inside and outside the ice ring.

Serves 10 to 12.

Elaine's Sangria

This simple recipe is refreshing and delicious. Pour a glass and enjoy on a hot summer day!

1 bottle dry red wine (such as Cabernet Sauvignon)

Orange juice with mango, such as Simply Orange brand

Sliced oranges

Sliced limes

Pour equal parts of red wine and juice into a pitcher.

Add sliced oranges and lime to pitcher for a nice presentation.

When ready to serve add ice to the pitcher and serve.

Pour sangria into individual glasses filled with ice.

Note: You can use any inexpensive dry red wine for this recipe.

BREAKFAST
AND SUCH

Spinach and Mushroom Crepes

These crepes are perfect for brunch or a holiday morning. They can be made ahead and frozen. Thaw completely before baking.

CREPES:

1 cup flour

1½ cup milk

3 eggs

Salt and pepper

2 Tbsp. melted butter, cooled

1 Tbsp. dried dill

MUSHROOM FILLING:

1 bunch green onions, minced

½ pound mushrooms, chopped

3 Tbsp. butter

2 pkgs. (10 oz. each) frozen chopped spinach, cooked briefly and squeezed dry

½ pound ham, diced

½ cup sour cream

Melted butter

Parmesan cheese

Salt and pepper

CREPES: Combine ingredients in food processor for 5 seconds. Let stand at room temperature for several hours or refrigerate overnight. Prepare crepes in a skillet. Be sure crepes are uniform in size.

FILLING: Sauté green onions and mushrooms in 3 tablespoons butter until golden. Add spinach, ham, and sour cream. Season to taste with salt and pepper. Mix well. Fill crepe, roll up and place in shallow greased casserole. Brush with melted butter and sprinkle with parmesan cheese. Cover with foil and bake at 350° for 20 minutes until heated.

Serves 6 to 8.

Breakfast Rellenos

Guests will love this. Good for a holiday morning or special brunch.

2 – 7 oz. cans whole green chilies, drained

9 large eggs

2 cups milk

½ cup flour

¼ tsp. garlic salt

¼ cup grated parmesan cheese

3.5 oz. can sliced black olives, drained

4 oz. can chopped green chilies

1 to 2 Tbsp. chopped jalapeño peppers (optional, and to taste)

¼ cup sliced green onions

¼ cup chopped fresh cilantro

8 oz. pkg. cream cheese, room temperature

¼ tsp. coarse ground pepper

Grease a 9 x 13-inch baking dish. Place whole green chilies, smooth side down, across bottom of pan. In a large bowl combine eggs, milk and flour and mix until frothy. Add remaining ingredients, blend well and pour over chilies. Bake at 375° for 45 minutes. Serve with a side of salsa.

Serves 10 to 12.

Buttermilk Pancakes

Fluffy, easy and great for Saturday morning. People have told me, "These are the best pancakes I've ever had."

3 eggs, separated

2 cups buttermilk

2 cups flour

1 tsp. baking soda

1 Tbsp. sugar

¼ cup unsalted butter, melted

Maple syrup

Butter for serving

Beat the egg yolks in a large bowl until light. Add the buttermilk and beat until smooth. Stir in the flour, baking soda and sugar until well mixed. Do not overbeat; the small lumps will disappear during cooking. Stir in the melted butter.

Beat the egg whites until stiff. Fold into the batter. Bake on a hot griddle, using about ⅓ cup batter for each pancake, until bubbles form on the top and the underside is nicely browned. Turn the cakes over and brown the other side.

Serve with plenty of butter and maple syrup.

Makes about 12 4-inch pancakes.

Zucchini Fritatta

This is a great breakfast or brunch recipe, especially when you have house guests. I make this in the morning and leave it out on the counter until lunchtime so that late risers can enjoy it when they wake up. Serve warm or at room temperature. If you have a favorite roll, such a ciabatta or croissant, put a slice of frittata in it for a terrific sandwich.

2 small zucchini (or 1 medium size zucchini)

1 medium onion, finely chopped

2 to 3 Tbsp. butter or extra virgin olive oil (or a combination of both)

12 eggs, beaten

2 Tbsp. fresh basil or 2 tsp. dried

2 tsp. salt

Cracked black pepper to taste

3 Tbsp. dried bread crumbs or dried cracker crumbs

1 cup grated cheddar cheese

½ cup high quality ham, diced (optional)

½ cup Parmesan cheese

Peel and shred zucchini (I use a handheld grater and grate over waxed paper). Sauté onion in butter and oil until soft. Add zucchini to onions and cook about 2 minutes. Remove from heat.

In a large bowl combine the beaten eggs, basil, salt and pepper. Fold in the onion and zucchini mixture, bread crumbs, shredded cheddar cheese, Parmesan cheese and ham. Pour into a buttered quiche dish and bake in a preheated 350° oven for 20 to 25 minutes or until eggs set. I insert a knife into the center of the quiche dish after about 20 minutes. If it comes out clean, it's done. If not, leave it in the oven and do the knife test every 2 minutes.

PIZZA AND BREAD

Grandma and Aunt Mary's Bread

Each week the Mogentale house would smell of freshly-baked bread. Loaf after loaf would emerge from the two ovens as the women continued to knead. Each loaf was wrapped in white butcher paper, tied with a string and used as a staple for the following week until it was time to bake again.

20 cups pre-sifted all-purpose flour

2 pkgs. active dry yeast (¼ oz.)

Warm water

½ cup sugar

2½ tsp. salt

⅓ cup Crisco shortening

8 cups warm water

In a very large bowl measure out pre-sifted flour. In a small bowl dissolve yeast in lukewarm water per yeast package directions.

To the flour add sugar, salt, Crisco, 8 cups warm water, and the dissolved yeast. Mix and knead all together about 20 to 25 minutes in a bread pan or bowl until smooth. Keep turning and kneading, sprinkling in additional flour as needed to get the right consistency. An additional 2 to 2½ cups of flour may be needed. The pan should come away clean and dough should be smooth, not sticky, and should make a nice ball.

Cover with a dish cloth and let rise to double in bulk. Dough should be kept warm. Cover over and under with a heavy tablecloth. It takes about an hour to rise. Push down the dough and let it come up a second time. This takes about 30 minutes. Mark the dough by cutting it in half, then each half into 4 pieces to make 8 loaves. Shape each piece into a loaf.

Grease bread pans with Crisco. Place shaped loaf in each pan. Cover with cloth and set aside and let rise to full pan. This takes about 1 hour.

Bake at 325° for about 45 minutes to 1 hour. The bread is done when it has a hollow sound when you tap it. Grease loaf with Crisco when you take it out of the oven. Place on cooling rack and thoroughly cool before wrapping for freezer.

Makes 8 loaves.

Garlic Bread

Simple garlic bread with fresh ingredients. A great accompaniment to any meal.

1 loaf fresh-baked Italian bread

2 sticks butter

8 to 10 cloves garlic, minced

Slowly melt butter in a medium saucepan until just melted. Add minced garlic. Over low heat let garlic gently sauté in the butter, being careful not to burn the butter or the garlic. Let garlic warm in melted butter for about 5 minutes.

Slice Italian bread with serrated knife. Take the heel of the bread and dip the cut side into the garlic butter. Place heel on a large piece of aluminum foil. Take next slice of bread and dip one cut side into garlic butter. Place slice next to heel on foil. Dip one side of each slice of bread into garlic butter and reconstruct the loaf on the aluminum foil sheet. Loosely wrap foil around the whole loaf of bread. Place in 250° oven for 10 to 20 minutes. Serve immediately.

Serves 6 to 8.

Savory Vegetable-Filled Bread

Pair this with the Sausage Bread for a picnic or hors d'oeuvres.

1 to 2 loaves frozen bread dough (or basic pizza dough recipe found in this book)

1 medium onion

6 cloves garlic, minced

1 medium eggplant or zucchini, minced

1 green pepper, minced

6 sundried tomatoes, soaked, drained and minced

2 Tbsp. tamari (or soy sauce)

½ cup water

1 Tbsp. dried basil

1 Tbsp. salt

Pinch of black pepper

If using frozen bread dough, let it thaw out and coat with a little oil. Cover dough and place in a warm area for 20 to 40 minutes. Prepare filling.

Chop veggies in food processor in order of their texture. Do not puree. Green pepper, onion, garlic, tomato, zucchini/eggplant. Combine all filling ingredients in a saucepan. Cook covered over medium heat for 10 minutes. Uncover and cook 5 minutes more to reduce liquid. Drain off any excess liquid.

Roll out dough into a rectangle and spread filling on entire surface of dough. Gently roll up and pinch edges closed. Place filled loaves onto a greased cookie sheet, cover with a clean towel and let rise for 30 minutes.

Bake in 375° oven for approximately 20 minutes, or until lightly brown.

Makes 1 to 2 loaves.

Sausage Bread

Great for a picnic, party or breakfast with eggs.

1 package Jimmy Dean sausage (mild or hot)

1 cup shredded cheddar cheese

1 cup shredded Monterey jack cheese

1 loaf frozen bread dough (or basic pizza dough recipe found in this book)

If using frozen bread dough let it thaw out and coat with a little oil. Cover and place in a warm area and let rise for 20 to 40 minutes.

While bread is thawing, fry sausage until done, breaking it up into small pieces. Drain sausage of grease and let cool. Roll out dough until ½ inch thick. Spread sausage and cheese over dough. Slowly roll up from one end to the other. DO NOT roll too tight. Brush top with melted butter. Bake at 350° for 30 minutes or until golden on top.

Serves 4 to 6.

BBQ Chicken Pizza

This recipe is one of my own. I don't generally order this when I'm out; however, I love making and eating this one in my own kitchen. Pair this with a fresh green salad.

1 recipe Basic Pizza Dough or store-bought pizza dough.

1 whole boneless, skinless chicken breast

1 – 8 oz. can tomato sauce

¼ cup KC Masterpiece Original BBQ sauce (or BBQ sauce of your choice)

½ cup fresh chopped cilantro

8 oz. package shredded mozzarella cheese

¼ cup red onion, sliced thin

Place chicken breast in a skillet and cover with water. Bring to a boil and simmer for 20 minutes. Season with salt and pepper. Let cool. Chop chicken breast into small pieces, or you can shred it.

Combine tomato sauce and BBQ sauce in a small bowl. Spread sauce mixture over surface of pizza dough. Top sauce with shredded chicken. Top chicken with mozzarella cheese. Top cheese with cilantro and onion slices. Bake in a preheated oven at 425° for 15 to 18 minutes until crust is lightly golden and cheese is melted. (If using store-bought crust follow baking directions on packaging.) Allow pizza to cool slightly before slicing.

Makes one nice pizza.

The Basic Pizza Dough recipe is included in this book. It's easy and faster than you'd think.

White Pizza with Roasted Garlic

Need an excuse to invite a few friends over? Make this and they'll come running. Pair this with your favorite wine.

2 heads garlic

2 tsp. olive oil

Salt and pepper

1 recipe Basic Pizza Dough or store-bought pizza dough

¼ cup extra virgin olive oil

3 to 4 oz. feta cheese

8 oz. package shredded mozzarella cheese

1 package fresh spinach (washed and cleaned)

Cut off top quarter of each of the garlic heads. Place garlic on a foil lined baking sheet. Drizzle with 2 teaspoons olive oil. Sprinkle lightly with salt and pepper. Turn garlic over, cut side down and bake for 1 hour in a 350° oven. Remove from oven and let cool until easy to handle.

Rough chop the spinach. Place in a colander over boiling water. Cover and steam for about 3 to 5 minutes. Remove spinach, set aside to cool slightly.

Squeeze each head of garlic into a bowl to remove the soft cloves. Add the ¼ cup of olive oil and mash it with the roasted garlic. Spread olive oil garlic mixture over pizza dough. Top with mozzarella cheese. Top mozzarella with steamed spinach. Top spinach with crumpled feta cheese. Bake in 425° oven for 18 minutes. (Or follow directions on package of purchased pizza dough). Remove from oven. Let rest 5 minutes before slicing.

Serves about 4 to 6.

Basic Pizza Dough

Simple and quick. Top this dough with traditional toppings or perhaps some unique alternatives. You may never order delivery again.

1 package active dry yeast (¼ oz.)

1 tsp. sugar

⅔ cup of warm water

1⅔ cups all-purpose flour

¾ tsp. salt

2 tsp. oil

1½ Tbsp. cornmeal for pan

Stir yeast and sugar into warm water and let stand until foamy, about 10 minutes. Insert metal blade into food processor. Put flour and salt in work bowl and turn on machine. Pour yeast mixture through feed tube and process about 45 seconds, until dough pulls away from sides of bowl. Add oil through feed tube and process 60 seconds longer.

If dough sticks to sides of bowl, add more flour, 1 tablespoon at a time, process for 10 seconds after each addition, until dough leaves sides of bowl but remains soft.

Place dough on a work surface. Let it rest for 5 minutes. Roll dough on floured surface into circle, rotating and turning dough often and using enough flour so it doesn't stick. Roll dough into a circle of approximately 15 inches. Sprinkle cornmeal over a baking stone (or lightly oil a baking sheet and sprinkle with cornmeal). Place dough onto prepared stone or baking sheet. Press into place from center outward, turn under 1 inch of outer part of dough to form a rim.

Pre-heat oven to 425°. Place pizza dough into pre-heated oven and bake for 6 minutes. Remove pizza from oven. Your pizza dough is now ready to fill with toppings.

Once you have place desired sauce and toppings on your pizza dough, place it back into the 425° oven and bake for 18 minutes, or until rim of crust is golden and bottom is brown.

Makes one large pizza dough.

SOUPS, SALADS, SAUCES AND CHILIS

Tomato Salad with Feta

1½ pounds cherry or grape tomatoes, halved

½ medium red onion, diced

¼ pound feta cheese, crumbled

2 ribs celery, chopped

2 Tbsp. olive oil

1 Tbsp. plus 1 tsp. white wine vinegar

1 tsp. fresh chopped oregano or ½ tsp. dried

Fresh cracked black pepper

Clove garlic, minced

In a large bowl, combine tomatoes, red onion, feta cheese and celery. In a small bowl, whisk together olive oil, vinegar, oregano, pepper and garlic. Pour dressing over vegetables; toss to coat well. Chill until ready to serve.

To serve, place on a platter and top with feta cheese.

Makes 6 servings.

Broccoli Salad

Cool, crisp and refreshing. This is always a crowd pleaser.

6 cups small broccoli florets

1 cup raisins

½ cup chopped onion

8 slices cooked, crisp bacon, crumbled

1½ cups shredded cheddar cheese

Toss ingredients for salad. Mix the dressing ingredients and add a sufficient amount to the salad to nicely moisten.

Serves 8.

DRESSING:

1 cup mayonnaise

½ cup granulated sugar

1 tablespoon vinegar

Black Bean and Corn Summer Salad

Very light and refreshing as an addition to any summer meal.

2 cups cooked black beans, or 1 – 15 oz. can black beans, drained and rinsed

1 Tbsp. olive oil

1 Tbsp. fresh lime juice

¼ cup picante sauce

½ tsp. salt

½ tsp. cumin

½ tsp. coriander

¼ cup red onion, finely chopped

½ cup red bell pepper, finely chopped

2 green onions, finely chopped

½ cup celery, finely chopped

½ cup carrots, finely chopped

½ cup fresh or frozen corn, cooked

½ to 1 whole avocado, chopped (optional)

2 tablespoons fresh cilantro, chopped

In a small bowl whisk together olive oil, lime juice, picante sauce, salt, cumin and coriander. In a large bowl gently combine vegetables and beans. Toss gently with dressing. Add avocado just before serving. Sprinkle with cilantro. Refrigerate until ready to serve.

This salad can be made one day ahead if necessary.

Serves 4 to 6.

Chicken Salad with a Twist

This salad can be served as a side dish or as a light lunch with a slice of hearty bread.

8 oz. uncooked corkscrew pasta

3 cups cooked chicken, cubed (about 4 breast halves)

½ cup Italian salad dressing

½ cup mayonnaise

3 Tbsp. lemon juice

1 Tbsp. yellow prepared mustard

1 medium onion, chopped

1 cup diced celery

1 tsp. ground black pepper

Salt to taste

Cook pasta and drain. Mix chicken and Italian dressing with hot pasta. Let cool. Blend mayonnaise, lemon juice and mustard. Stir in onions, celery, salt and pepper. Add to pasta mixture and mix well. Chill at least 2 hours before serving.

Serves 6 to 8.

Couscous with Almonds & Feta

1½ cups water

1 cup couscous

3 Tbsp. olive oil

3 Tbsp. lemon juice

¼ cup toasted slivered
almonds

½ cup diced tomatoes

3 oz. or more feta cheese

¼ cup sweet onion, minced

Lots of fresh mint, chopped

In a medium saucepan, bring water to
a boil. Add some salt and stir in the
couscous. Turn off heat and add olive oil.
Toss and transfer to a larger serving bowl.
Add all ingredients; mix and enjoy.

Serves 6 to 8.

Taco Salad

A casual, refreshing salad.

1 pound lean ground beef, browned in skillet

12 oz. bag shredded cheddar cheese

1 bunch green onions, chopped

½ cup frozen peas, thawed

1 small head iceberg lettuce, chopped

1 can black olives, sliced

1 cup tortilla chips, crushed

1 bottle Catalina salad dressing (light or fat-free is fine)

Sour cream

Mix first 6 ingredients together. Add crushed chips and dressing just before serving. Toss and serve. Top each serving with a dollop of sour cream.

Serves 4 to 6.

NOTE: I cook the meat in advance and chop all other ingredients in advance before we go to the lake each summer. I store each ingredient separately in plastic zip bags. This saves me a lot of time and clean-up. When it's time to prepare the salad, I simply dump all of the contents into one bowl. Crush the chips over the top. Add the dressing and stir.

Rainbow JELL-O Salad

This layered salad is made and shared every year at Thanksgiving and Christmas. It is a tradition that Jack's children will likely continue for years to come. It is not only delicious–it is beautiful.

1½ pints sour cream

6 – 3 oz. pkgs of JELL-O

Flavors:
1. Black Cherry
2. Lemon
3. Strawberry
4. Orange
5. Lime
6. Raspberry

Mix one package of JELL-O (start with the Black Cherry) with 1 cup boiling water; divide into 2 equal parts. Whisk together ⅓ cup sour cream to one part and ¼ cup of hot water to the other. Start with the sour cream layer (skim off bubbles before putting into pan) and spoon into a 9 x 13-inch glass dish.

Refrigerate half an hour then spoon on the plain layer. (You can leave the plain layer on the counter until ready) Repeat this process for each flavor of JELL-O.

This salad will take at least 6 hours to complete but only takes a few minutes each time and can be made over several days.

Cranberry Holiday Salad

Your guests will never know this delicious salad is mostly sugar-free. It is refreshing and perfect when paired with ham or turkey.

1 – 8oz. box sugar-free JELL-O pudding, vanilla (do not use instant pudding)

1 – 3 oz. box sugar-free lemon JELL-O

1 – 3 oz. box sugar-free raspberry JELL-O

2 cups cold water

1 cup boiling water

1 Tbsp. lemon juice

1 – 1 pound can whole cranberry sauce

¼ cup pecans, chopped

6 Tbsp. celery, diced fine

½ of 1-pound carton Cool Whip topping

Pinch of nutmeg

Combine pudding, lemon JELL-O and 2 cups cold water in a sauce pan. Heat to medium and stir constantly until mixture begins to boil. Stir in lemon juice and chill until partially set.

In a small bowl dissolve raspberry JELL-O in the cup of boiling water and cool. Mix in cranberries, nuts and celery. Chill until partially set.

When the pudding/lemon JELL-O mixture is partially set, stir in the Cool Whip and nutmeg. When well-mixed pour half of the pudding mixture into an 8 x 8-inch square glass baking dish. Carefully pour the slightly thickened cranberry mixture over the top. Top with remaining pudding mixture. Chill overnight.

Serves 6 to 8.

Macaroni Salad

This is one of George's forever-favorite salads. The key is to smash the hard boiled eggs with the back tines of the fork as well as chopping or grating the onion very finely.

16 oz. package of pasta (elbow or try a different shape such as campanelle or casarecce)

1 cup celery, chopped

¼ cup onion, grated or finely chopped (use more onion if you'd like)

4 hard-boiled eggs, mashed

½ red bell pepper, chopped small

DRESSING:

1 cup mayonnaise (I use light mayonnaise)

3 Tbsp. apple cider vinegar

Salt & pepper to taste

Cook pasta al dente. Mix all of the dressing ingredients. When pasta has slightly cooled, add the dressing, celery, onion, mashed eggs and bell pepper. Mix thoroughly and refrigerate.

Albondigas Soup

Terrific meatball soup

¾ cup white rice

1½ cups water

4 Tbsp. vegetable oil

2 white onions, diced

1 pound lean ground beef

1 egg

1 tsp. ground cumin

1 tsp. dried oregano

1½ tsp. salt

1 tsp. freshly ground pepper

1 clove garlic, minced

1 zucchini, diced

2 carrots, peeled and diced

2 ripe tomatoes, peeled, seeded and diced

6 cups chicken stock

Place rice in a heatproof bowl. Bring the water to a boil and pour over the rice. Let soak for 40 minutes, then drain; set aside.

In a sauté pan over medium heat, warm 2 tablespoons of vegetable oil. Add 1 of the onions and sauté until soft. Remove from heat and let cool.

In a bowl, combine the beef, cooled onion, soaked rice, egg, cumin, oregano, ¾ teaspoon of the salt and ½ teaspoon of the pepper. Using your hands, mix well and form into 1-inch balls.

In a large soup pot over medium heat, warm the remaining 2 tablespoons of oil. Add the remaining onion and sauté until soft. Add the garlic, zucchini, carrots and tomatoes and cook, stirring until fragrant, about 5 minutes. Add the chicken stock, stir well and bring to a boil. Carefully slip the meatballs into the pot, reduce the heat and simmer uncovered until the meatballs are fully cooked, about 45 minutes. Do not stir during this time; only shake the pot gently to move the balls about. Add salt and pepper to taste.

Ladle soup into bowls and top with grated parmesan cheese.

Makes 6 to 8 servings.

Italian Wedding Soup

Traditional and delicious. Hard to find in restaurants in the Midwest, whereas it is a staple in many Italian restaurants in the east.

2 cups celery, finely diced (about 4 stalks from the bunch)

1 small onion, finely diced

1½ cups carrots, finely diced (about 3 carrots)

I head escarole or spinach (about 1 pound) small rough-chopped

2 whole boneless, skinless chicken breasts.

2 – 48 oz. cans of good quality chicken stock (about 10 cups)

½ cup dry acini di pepe pasta

MEATBALLS:

12 oz. ground veal or ground beef or combination

4 Tbsp. grated parmesan cheese

2 Tbsp. bread crumbs

¼ cup milk

1 Tbsp. fresh chopped parsley

¼ tsp. salt

1/8 tsp. pepper

1 clove garlic, crushed and minced

¼ tsp. dried oregano

¼ tsp. dried basil

Combine meatball ingredients and form small meat balls, about ½ inch in diameter. Simmer the small balls in salted water about 2 or 3 minutes. Drain meatballs and refrigerate until needed.

Put chicken stock in a large stock pot and bring to a boil. Add chicken breasts and simmer about 20 minutes until chicken is cooked through. Strain chicken from stock and reserve. In another stock pot sauté celery, carrots and onions in a little oil until tender about 10 minutes. Carefully add stock. Bring to low boil and add pasta, escarole and meatballs. Simmer 10 minutes.

Cut or pull apart cooked chicken breasts into small pieces. Add chicken pieces into soup. Simmer about 10 minutes. Serve soup with lots of fresh grated parmesan cheese and chopped parsley.

Serves 10 to 12.

Rice Milk Soup

This simple soup makes a great meal. It's thick, delicious and filling. My great aunt Mary, who was also my godmother, often made this soup for me when I was young. I then made it for my son. This soup brings back great memories.

1 cup rice

1 Tbsp. Butter

½ gallon milk (or more for desired consistency)

Salt

Melt butter and add rice, coat rice with butter. As rice begins to get hot, continue stirring and slowly add milk one cup at a time. As you continue to stir and the mixture begins to thicken add another cup of milk. Continue this process of adding milk and stirring until rice is cooked and tender and until soup has reached your desired thickness. Season with salt.

If you get tired of stirring and watching, simply add 2 cups of milk, stir until it becomes hot to avoid rice sticking to bottom then cover with lid and turn off stove. Check soup in about 20 minutes. Add more milk if necessary and repeat process.

Makes about 4 to 6 cups.

Lettiann's Award-winning Chili

Make a batch and invite some friends over.

1 pound ground turkey breast

1 pound Italian sausage, loose*

1 large onion, chopped

1 green pepper, chopped

2 cloves garlic, minced

1 – 28oz. can crushed Italian tomatoes

1 – 15 oz. can tomato sauce

1 – 6 oz. can tomato paste

3 – 15 oz. cans dark red kidney beans, drained and rinsed

1 cup water

1 jar Heinz chili sauce

1 Tbsp. chili powder, or more to taste

1 tsp. cumin

½ tsp. cinnamon

1 Tbsp. sugar

Brown turkey and sausage. Add chopped onion, green pepper and garlic. Sauté over medium heat, stirring constantly, about 3 to 5 minutes. Add crushed tomatoes, tomato sauce, tomato paste and water. Stir to incorporate. Add spices and add chili sauce. Cook over low heat, covered, about 2 hours. Stir occasionally. Drain and rinse kidney beans. Add beans and sugar to chili. Enjoy.

Makes a big batch. Leftovers? Freeze 'em.

Serves 8 to 10.

*Can use Italian turkey sausage, if you prefer.

Cincinnati Chili

Very popular in Cincinnati and, after you try it, it may be a favorite of yours as well. I can't be in Ohio without stopping at a Skyline Chili restaurant. This recipe is my version.

1 quart water

2 medium-sized onions, grate fine

2 – 8 oz. cans tomato sauce

5 whole allspice (or 1 tsp. ground)

½ tsp. crushed red pepper

1 tsp. ground cumin

4 Tbsp. chili powder

½ oz. bitter chocolate

2 pounds ground beef

4 cloves garlic, minced

2 Tbsp. vinegar

1 large bay leaf, whole

5 whole cloves (or 1 tsp. ground)

2 tsp. Worcestershire sauce

1½ tsp. salt

1 tsp. cinnamon

Add ground beef to water in large stock pot; stir until beef separates to a fine texture. Boil slowly for 30 minutes. Add all other ingredients. Stir to blend, bringing to boil; reduce heat and simmer covered for about 3 hours. Stir occasionally. Remove cover during last hour until desired consistency is reached.

Serve it in one of the following traditional styles:

Chili plain

Chili and spaghetti

3 way – chili, spaghetti and shredded cheddar cheese

4 way – chili, spaghetti, cheese and chopped onions

5 way – chili, spaghetti, cheese, onions and beans

Coney Island – a frankfurter in a bun topped with chili, cheese and onions or any of the above combinations.

Lettiann's Meat Sauce

In high school while my friends were shopping at the mall for clothes, I was in the nearest kitchen store buying a wok or a heat-proof spatula. Often on Sundays after Mass, I would piddle in the kitchen trying to come up with the perfect meat sauce for the pasta. I make a large batch, let it simmer all afternoon, put it into containers and keep it in the freezer. The sauce never stays in the freezer very long.

1 large onion, chopped

1 Tbsp. extra virgin olive oil

½ stick butter

1½ pounds lean ground beef

2 tsp. dried oregano

2 tsp. dried basil

4 cloves garlic, minced

1 Tbsp. sugar

1 tsp. salt

½ tsp. black pepper

3 – 28 oz. cans crushed tomatoes (or in summer time I use fresh, peeled tomatoes)

2 – 6 oz. cans tomato paste

1 cup water

½ cup fresh parsley, chopped

Put olive oil and butter in a stock pot on the stove over medium heat. As butter is melting add onions and sauté for 5 minutes. Be careful not to let butter burn. Stir in oregano, basil and garlic. Stir quickly about 1 minute; do not allow the garlic to brown. Remove sautéed onions from heat and put in a separate bowl. Using the same stock pot, brown ground beef until cooked through. Then add the onion/herb mixture back into the stock pot with the beef. Gently add the crushed tomatoes, tomato paste, water, sugar, salt, pepper and fresh parsley. Stir over medium heat until almost boiling. Reduce heat to simmer and partially cover pot with a lid. Allow sauce to simmer at least 2 hours so that flavors incorporate.

Serve with your favorite pasta.

Makes about 8 cups.

Allow sauce to cool before putting into containers. Remember, sauce tastes even better the next day.

Lettiann's Sunday Sauce

Italian red sauce. Spaghetti sauce. Tomato sauce. Whatever you'd like to call it. I call it delicious and versatile.

1 large onion, finely chopped

2 Tbsp. extra virgin olive oil

2 Tbsp. butter

6 to 8 garlic cloves, minced

2 Tbsp. dried basil

3 – 28 oz. cans crushed tomatoes

1 – 6 oz. can of tomato paste

1 cup water*

1 tsp. dried oregano

2 tsp. salt

1 tsp. black pepper

Sauté onions in olive oil and butter over medium heat until soft. Add fresh minced garlic and dried basil. Continue cooking gently for 2 minutes. Add the crushed tomatoes, tomato paste and water. Stir to combine. Add oregano, salt and pepper. Bring sauce to a boil, reduce heat to simmer, cover and cook for 1 to 2 hours, stirring occasionally.

This sauce freezes well.

Rinse crushed tomato and tomato paste with water then put that water into the sauce.

Creamy Blue Cheese Dressing

Right alongside the steaming hot lasagna were individual salads, each with a huge dollop of homemade blue cheese dressing.

4 oz. crumbled blue cheese

1 cup (8 oz.) sour cream

½ cup (4 oz.) mayonnaise

¼ cup buttermilk
(can substitute milk, if
necessary)

Juice of ½ lemon

½ tsp. white wine vinegar

½ tsp. Worcestershire sauce

¼ cup red onion, rough-
chopped

Salt and black pepper

Combine all ingredients in a food processer. Pulse all ingredients quickly, just enough to incorporate. Dressing should have texture, not processed until smooth.

Makes about 2 cups.

SIDE DISHES

Grandma Larson's Corn Pudding

Yes, here it is. The long awaited Southerland/Larson family recipe that no one could find. Thank you Aunt Laurie for finding and forwarding this ever-talked-about family-favorite recipe.

4 eggs

1 – 16 oz. can cream-style corn

3 Tbsp. flour

1 Tbsp. sugar

1 tsp. salt

Dash pepper

1 cup milk or light cream

1 Tbsp. melted butter

Beat eggs until thick. Mix in corn. In separate bowl, combine flour, sugar, salt and pepper. Very slowly blend into milk or cream. Mix in melted butter. Combine with corn mixture. Pour into greased 1½ quart casserole.

Bake at 325° for 1 hour. Aunt Laurie likes to put a little whole corn (unblended) on the top for a heartier casserole.

Serves 6.

Green Bean Bundles

Somewhere in the Larson/Southerland family this recipe was written down. My husband made them for a Christmas dinner one year and when he mentioned the ingredients I was curious what it would taste like. It was really good. Bravo, Jack.

2 cans whole green beans, drained and rinsed

Bacon strips—not thick

Catalina salad dressing

Pour the Catalina dressing into a 9 x 13-inch baking dish. Wrap bacon around 5 to 6 whole green beans and fasten with a toothpick. Bacon can be cut in half. Cover with foil. Bake at 325° for 20 to 30 minutes. Remove foil and bake an additional 20 to 30 minutes or until crisp.

Serves 8.

Pitt Potatoes

A friend of mine makes this fabulous "Pitt" potatoes recipe for his customers in Pittsburgh, Pennsylvania. These popular potatoes are the most requested side dish on his menu.

10 pounds white potatoes, skins brushed clean

¼ cup garlic, chopped (use fresh)

3 green peppers, chopped

2 to 3 onions, chopped

2 pounds kielbasa, cut into bit-size pieces

1½ Tbsp. salt

1 Tbsp. ground pepper

¼ cup parsley, chopped

1 Tbsp. dried oregano

3 sticks butter

Cut the potatoes into bite-size pieces with the skin on (too small will make them mushy). Spray a roasting pan (either electric or one you can put into the oven) with vegetable cooking spray and turn to 350°. Melt 1½ sticks of butter on the roaster. Add only the potatoes and mix until all are coated with butter. Cook potatoes for about 45 minutes. After potatoes have cooked alone for 45 minutes add the chopped green peppers, onions, kielbasa, all seasonings and the remaining 1½ sticks of butter (cut into slices). Incorporate all ingredients gently. Continue to cook at 350° for another 40 minutes. Reduce heat to 250° and cook for an additional 30 minutes or until potatoes, peppers and onions are tender.

Serves about 16 to 18 as a side dish. This recipe can easily be halved.

Cowboy Beans

They'll keep coming back for more of these popular beans.

½ lb. bacon, chopped

1 large onion, chopped

1½ lbs. ground beef

½ cup brown sugar, packed

½ cup ketchup

1 Tbsp. yellow mustard

1 Tbsp. vinegar

2 cans (15 oz. each) kidney beans, drained and rinsed

2 cans (15 oz. each) butter beans, drained and rinsed

2 cans (28 oz. each) baked beans, DO NOT drain or rinse

Brown chopped bacon until crisp. Add onion and ground beef. Cook until done. Mix brown sugar, ketchup, mustard and vinegar in a large bowl and then add the meat mixture. Add beans, folding gently.

Put into a baking dish and bake at 350° for 1 hour.

Serves 10.

Zucchini Pancakes Marinara

4 medium zucchini, washed and trimmed

1 large carrot, washed, peeled and trimmed

½ tsp. salt

1 Tbsp. lemon juice

1 green onion, finely chopped

2 cloves garlic, crushed or minced

2 eggs

½ cup flour

2 tsp. dried basil

¼ cup parmesan cheese

½ Tbsp. ground black pepper

2 Tbsp. olive oil

2 cups of your favorite marinara sauce

Shred zucchini and carrot on the larger holes of a cheese grater or using the shredder attachment on a food processor. Place in colander and sprinkle with salt. Toss lightly and allow to stand for 10 minutes. Squeeze vegetables between your fingers to expel any excess moisture. Transfer to a large bowl. Add lemon juice, green onions, garlic and eggs.

In a separate bowl, combine flour, basil, parmesan cheese and pepper. Stir to blend well, then stir into vegetables.

Heat 1 tablespoon of the oil on a nonstick griddle or in a large nonstick skillet set over medium-high heat. Spoon ¼ cup of batter for each pancake and cook about 3 to 4 minutes per side. Add oil only as needed to keep each batch from sticking.

If desired keep pancakes warm in a 250° oven. Serve topped with your favorite tomato sauce.

Makes 4 servings of 3 pancakes each.

Creamy Corn & Cheese Bake

Everybody wants seconds of this terrific side dish.

1 can corn

1 can cream-style corn

½ stick butter, softened

1 egg

1 can chopped green chilies (optional)

1 box cornbread mix (such as Jiffy brand)

¾ cup milk

1 cup shredded cheddar cheese

Combine all ingredients together in a large bowl. Put into 9 x 13-inch baking dish and bake for 45 minutes in a pre-heated 350° oven.

Serve 6 to 8.

Yellow Rice Salad with Roasted Peppers and Spicy Black Beans

Great side dish, especially with fish and chicken

4 tsp. ground cumin

¼ cup fresh lime juice

2½ tablespoons vegetable oil

½ teaspoon turmeric

2 cups water

1 cup basmati or white rice

1 tsp. salt

½ cup thinly sliced green onions

1 – 15 oz. can black beans, rinsed and drained

½ cup chopped roasted red peppers from jar

½ cup chopped green bell pepper

⅓ cup chopped fresh cilantro

1½ tsp. canned chipotle chilies, minced

Stir 3 teaspoons cumin in small dry skillet over medium heat, just until fragrant, about 1 minute. Remove from heat. Whisk lime juice and oil into skillet.

In separate saucepan stir remaining cumin and turmeric over medium heat until fragrant, about 1 minute. Add 2 cups water, rice and salt; bring to boil. Reduce heat to low and cover; simmer until water is absorbed, about 15 minutes. Cool rice. Mix onions and half of the dressing into rice. Season with salt and pepper.

Combine black beans, all peppers, cilantro, chipotle chilies and remaining dressing in medium bowl. Toss to coat. Season with salt and pepper.

Gently mix bean mixture with rice. Place in a decorative serving dish.

Serve immediately. This is served at room temperature. Don't worry about serving it hot.

Serves 4 to 6.

Tasty Mashed Potatoes

A great combination makes these rich, tasty potatoes.

4 to 6 Idaho potatoes

¼ cup sour cream

¼ cup butter

¼ cup cubed Velveeta cheese

Salt and pepper

Depending on the quantity of potatoes you're using, you may need more than ¼ cup of each ingredient. Use equal amounts of sour cream, Velveeta and butter, adjusting the amounts to your taste. You can't go wrong.

Peel potatoes and cut them into large cubes. Place potatoes in a stock pot and cover with water. Bring to a boil. Reduce to medium heat, partially cover and let cook for 12 to 15 minutes. Pierce with fork to make sure potatoes are tender. Remove from stove and drain liquid. Return potatoes to the stock pot. Add the sour cream, Velveeta and butter. Add salt and pepper to taste. Put the lid on, return pot to stove and let ingredients melt. Be sure burner is turned off.

At this time, I generally finish the main dish. Just before serving, remove lid from pot and mash the potatoes, incorporating all of the melted ingredients. You can use a hand-held mixer or mash by hand. The mashed potatoes are now ready for serving.

TIP: On occasion I've added a tablespoon or two of prepared horseradish. Use your imagination.

Serves 8.

PASTA

Aglio e Olio

Italian for "garlic and oil." This simple dish is so delicious. This was the first meal that I made for my husband when we were first dating. He said to me, "How did you whip up something so good out of nothing?" Aunt Letty always called it "Aglio e Olio"—Jack and I now refer to it as "pasta with spinach and feta."

5 to 8 cloves garlic, minced

⅓ cup extra virgin olive oil

4 Tbsp. butter

1 pound (16 oz.) linguini

1 pound (16 oz.) fresh spinach

Red pepper flakes, crushed

Pine nuts, roasted

Parmesan cheese, grated

Salt and pepper, to taste

Feta cheese, crumbled

In a large skillet, gently sauté garlic in olive oil and butter over low-to-medium heat, being careful not to burn. When garlic is soft, remove from heat and add ½ teaspoon crushed red pepper flakes. Meanwhile, in a separate stock pot, boil water (with a tablespoon of salt) and add the pasta.

Before the pasta is finished cooking, ladle out one cup of pasta water and add to the skillet with the sautéed garlic, red pepper and oil. Return skillet to medium heat.

When linguini has cooked about 6 minutes and is still firm to the touch, using a pair of tongs, remove the pasta directly from the stock pot and add to the sauce in the skillet. Return to a simmer. The pasta will finish cooking here for a minute or so. Gently toss to coat. After 1 to 2 minutes, adjust the seasonings, adding more crushed pepper, salt and pepper, if needed.

In a separate sauté pan, add 1 tablespoon of olive oil and place over medium heat. Add the fresh spinach. Toss the spinach until it just starts to wilt. Season with black pepper. Remove from heat.

Place pasta into individual bowls or serving dishes. Add desired topping to pasta. The following are our individual topping preferences. What might yours be?

Lettiann: Parmesan cheese, roasted pine nuts, sautéed spinach and feta

Jack: sautéed spinach, roasted pine nuts, feta and Sriracha sauce

Nick: sautéed spinach, feta, Sriracha sauce and cottage cheese

Gnocchi (Potato)

Have you really had Gnocchi? I mean homemade potato pasta smothered in a homemade meat sauce? It is truly a treat. I never realized how much work actually went into the production of these tiny bundles of deliciousness until I made them by myself. My grandmother and aunts put a lot of love (and work) into all of their food.

4 pounds Idaho potatoes

4½ cups all-purpose flour

4 eggs, beaten

1½ tsp. salt

Bring a large pot of water to a boil. Cook the potatoes with their skin on in the boiling water for about 12 minutes or until soft. Drain and remove the skins of the potatoes. Place potatoes through a ricer.

Add the flour (hold back ½ cup), the eggs and salt. Beat to incorporate into a soft dough. Turn dough out onto a work surface and knead it gently about 3 minutes. Use a little of the ½ cup of reserved flour on the work board.

Pull off a lump of dough and roll into a long roll about 1 inch in diameter. Cut into pieces ¾ of an inch long and roll the gnocchi gently over the tines of a fork, making each one ridged. Place a little flour on a cloth and place the cut gnocchi on the cloth until all have been rolled and cut, and now you are ready to cook them.

Bring a large pot of water to a boil. Drop about 15 gnocchi at a time in the boiling water and cook 2 to 3 minutes until the gnocchi rise to the top of the water. Remove with a slotted spoon, draining well. Place in a casserole dish as you cook each batch.

Pour on your favorite meat sauce and cover with parmesan cheese. You can the heat in the oven at 350° for 15 or 20 minutes, covered.

NOTE: Gnocchi are also good served with melted butter and parmesan cheese, or gorgonzola cream sauce.

Recipe makes about 25 dozen.

Homemade Manicotti & Filling

CREPES:

6 eggs, room temperature

1½ cup flour

¼ tsp. salt

1½ cups water

FILLING:

2 pounds ricotta cheese

1 egg

6 oz. mozzarella cheese, diced or shredded

⅓ cup fresh grated parmesan cheese

½ tsp. salt

¼ tsp. ground black pepper

3 Tbsp. fresh chopped parsley

Marinara sauce

FOR CREPES: Combine crepe ingredients in an electric mixer, beat until smooth. Let stand for ½ hour or more. Heat 8-inch nonstick skillet and pour 3 tablespoons batter, rotating to spread. Cook until dry. Do not brown and only cook on one side. Cool and stack between waxed paper.

FOR FILLING: Blend all ingredients well in a large bowl with a wooden spoon. Spread about ¼ cup down center of crepe. Roll up. Spoon marinara sauce in bottom of baking dish. Place manicotti, seam side down. Cover with sauce and cheese. Bake uncovered ½ hour or until bubbly in a 350° oven.

NOTE: Manicotti can be rolled and then frozen. Place rolled manicotti on a greased cookie sheet in freezer. When frozen, remove from cookie sheet and store in plastic freezer bags. If frozen, thaw manicotti first before baking.

Makes about 3 dozen.

Lasagna

This is the classic lasagna my mother would prepare. She would serve this lasagna with a mixed green salad and her homemade chunky blue cheese dressing along with mouthwatering garlic bread. "Oh, what a meal."

RICOTTA MIXTURE:

1 – 15 oz. container ricotta cheese

1 egg

½ cup fresh parsley, chopped

Salt and pepper

Dash of garlic powder

1 package dry lasagna noodles

1 pound shredded mozzarella

1 pound shredded provolone

1 recipe meat sauce found in this book (or your favorite red sauce)

Fresh grated parmesan cheese

Cook lasagna noodles according to directions on package (do not overcook noodles), drain. Mix together ingredients for ricotta mixture.

In assembly line fashion arrange the following in a 9 x 13-inch, baking pan:

Cover bottom of lasagna pan with a thin layer of meat sauce or tomato sauce;

Place a single layer of lasagna noodles over sauce to cover;

Top noodles with an even spread of the ricotta mixture;

Sprinkle a large handful of mozzarella and provolone over top ricotta mixture;

Gently spread another layer of meat sauce over cheeses and repeat layering of ingredients as stated above;

Final layer should be cheeses then sprinkle the top with freshly grated parmesan cheese.

Bake in 350° oven for 1 to 1½ hours, until hot and bubbly. Let rest 10 to 15 minutes before cutting as pieces will stay together better. This freezes well, but be sure to defrost thoroughly in refrigerator before baking.

Serves 10 to 12.

Pasta with Black Bean Sauce

I stumbled over this recipe many years ago. It has been one of my favorites ever since.

1 medium onion, coarsely chopped

1 clove garlic, minced

1 Tbsp. vegetable oil

1 – 15 oz. can black beans, rinsed and drained

2 – 15 oz. cans stewed tomatoes (do not drain)

½ cup picante sauce

1 tsp. chili powder

1 tsp. ground cumin

¼ tsp. oregano, crushed

1 pound of your favorite pasta

Shredded cheddar or Colby-Jack cheese

Cook onion and garlic in oil in large skillet until onion is tender. Stir in remaining ingredients except pasta; bring to a boil. Reduce heat, cover and simmer 15 minutes, stirring occasionally. Uncover; cook over medium high heat until desired consistency. Serve bean mixture over pasta. Top with shredded cheese and perhaps a dollop of sour cream.

Makes 4 servings.

Italian Stuffed Shells with Spinach

1 – 12 oz. package jumbo stuffing pasta shells, uncooked

1 – 15 oz. container ricotta cheese

1 egg, beaten

½ cup grated parmesan cheese

Pinch of garlic powder

½ tsp. salt

½ tsp. pepper

3 to 4 cups tomato sauce, preferably homemade

1 cup fresh spinach, blanched, drained and rough chopped (optional)

2 cups (about 8 oz.) shredded mozzarella cheese

Prepare pasta shells according to package directions; drain.

Whip together ricotta, egg, parmesan, 1 cup of shredded mozzarella, garlic powder, salt and pepper. Stir in spinach, if using.

Fill shells equally with cheese mixture. Pour 2 cups of the tomato sauce in a 9 x 13-inch baking dish. Arrange shells on sauce, and pour remaining sauce over shells.

Cover; bake in 350° oven for 25 minutes. Uncover and top with remaining mozzarella. Cover; return to oven for about 10 to 15 minutes.

Enjoy this meal with some hearty Italian bread and a fresh green salad.

Serves about 6.

Pastitso

Greek Macaroni and meat. Don't wait for the Greek festival—you can enjoy this anytime of the year.

1 large onion, grated

¼ pound butter

2 pounds ground meat

1 tsp. salt

¼ tsp. black pepper

½ tsp. cinnamon

4 Tbsp. tomato paste

½ cup water

1 egg

MACARONI:

1 pound elbow macaroni

3 eggs, beaten

1¾ cups grated Romano cheese

WHITE SAUCE:

¼ pound butter

½ cup flour

3 cups milk

5 egg yolks

¼ cup grated Romano cheese

Brown onion in butter. Add meat, stirring until meat is brown. Add salt, pepper, cinnamon, tomato paste and water. Cook, uncovered, over medium heat about 20 minutes, stirring occasionally until water is absorbed. Remove from heat and cool. Beat egg very well and add to meat mixture.

MACARONI: Cook macaroni 8 minutes in boiling salted water. Rinse under hot water and drain. Toss macaroni with beaten eggs and cheese.

WHITE SAUCE: Melt butter. Add flour and mix well. Gradually add cold milk, stir well. Cook until thick, stirring often. Remove from heat. After 5 minutes, while sauce is cooling, beat egg yolks very well and blend into sauce. Add cheese.

Butter a 10 x 14-inch pan. Put ½ of macaroni mix in pan. Put meat mixture over macaroni, spreading evenly. Put rest of macaroni on top, also spreading evenly. Put white sauce all over top. Bake at 375° for 45 minutes or until golden brown. (Bake a bit longer if you had to refrigerate the pestitso before baking).

Serves 10 to 12.

MAIN DISHES

Braised Short Ribs of Beef

Terrific dish that can be prepared while you're at work. Serve over a bed of white basmati rice with a green salad.

2 pounds boneless beef short ribs, cut into 2-inch cubes

1 Tbsp. chili garlic sauce*

1 Tbsp. hoisin sauce

½ cup soy sauce

2 Tbsp. brown sugar

2 cloves garlic, chopped

¼ cup green onions, chopped

Combine chili garlic sauce, hoisin sauce, soy sauce, brown sugar, chopped garlic and green onions in bowl, stirring to combine. Place cubed short ribs into a crock pot. Pour sauce over meat. Cook in crock pot for 6 hours on medium heat. Serve beef over a bed of white rice.

Chili garlic sauce is available at Asian markets and some grocery stores.

Serves 4.

Rare Beef Tenderloin

A fantastic main dish for special occasions. I usually serve this at holiday time. Don't let the odd preparation fool you. This tenderloin is first class.

½ cup dark rum

½ cup soy sauce

5 to 6 pounds beef tenderloin

Combine rum and soy sauce to make marinade. Pour over tenderloin. Marinate in refrigerator for 12 hours.

Drain marinade and reserve. Preheat oven to 425°. Bake tenderloin for 20 minutes. Reduce heat to 300° and bake 15 minutes longer. Refrigerate in marinade for another 12 to 24 hours.

Drain marinade and reserve. Cook meat on grill for 15 minutes over medium heat. Heat reserve marinade to boil. The reserve marinade must be boiled before serving with cooked meat.

Use marinade as a sauce and pour it over tenderloin before serving.

Serves 10 to 12.

Beef Rib Roast

This makes a spectacular main course for a special occasion. Purchase your beef rib roast from a trusted butcher as a good cut of meat can make the biggest difference.

6 to 8 pounds beef rib roast (2 to 4 ribs), small end

SEASONING:

2 Tbsp. minced fresh parsley

1 Tbsp. dried thyme leaves, crushed

1 Tbsp. vegetable oil

2 tsp. cracked black pepper

4 cloves garlic, crushed

Creamy horseradish and chive sauce

(Sauce recipe below— Prepare this sauce the day before.)

Heat oven to 350°. In small bowl combine seasoning ingredients. Press evenly into surface of beef roast.

Place roast fat side up in shallow roasting pan. Insert ovenproof meat thermometer so tip is centered in thickest part, not resting on fat or touching bone. Do not add water. Roast 2¼ to 2½ hours for medium rare; 2¾ to 3 hours for medium doneness.

Remove roast when meat thermometer registers 135° for medium rare; 150° for medium doneness. Transfer roast to carving board; tent loosely with aluminum foil. Let stand for 15 minutes. Carve roast. Serve with horseradish sauce.

CREAMY HORSERADISH AND CHIVE SAUCE: In a medium bowl combine two cups of sour cream, ½ cup prepared horseradish, ⅓ cup milk, 2 tablespoons chopped fresh chives and ¼ teaspoon ground white pepper. Cover and refrigerate sauce until ready to serve.

Makes 8 to 10 servings.

Apple-Glazed Beef Brisket

First prize winner in the National Beef Cook-off. The winner was Vicki Wadlington of Tennessee.

4 to 5 pound boneless beef brisket, trimmed

1 medium onion, quartered

2 large garlic cloves, halved

10 whole cloves

Water

1 jar (10 oz.) apple jelly

⅓ cup dry white wine

3 Tbsp. Dijon-style mustard

3 Tbsp. minced green onions, including tops

1½ tsp. salt

¾ tsp. cracked black pepper

¾ tsp. curry powder

Fresh parsley for garnish

Place brisket, onion, garlic and cloves in a large Dutch oven or stock pot. Add water to cover. Bring to boil, reduce heat, cover and simmer 2½ to 3 hours or until tender. Drain brisket, cover and refrigerate up to 24 hours.

To prepare glaze, combine apple jelly, wine, mustard, green onions, salt, pepper and curry powder in small sauce pan and heat until jelly melts, stirring occasionally.

Place brisket in a shallow roasting pan. Brush with glaze and roast in slow oven (325°) for 45 minutes to 1 hour, basting frequently with glaze. Carve brisket into thin slices. Place brisket onto serving platter. Pour remaining glaze over brisket (make sure glaze is hot from the stove), and garnish with fresh parsley.

NOTE: Brisket can also be cooked on the charcoal grill for 30 minutes, basting often with glaze. (Be sure to first cook the brisket in the stock pot of water over the stove.)

Serves 8.

BBQ Beef Brisket

Great do-ahead dinner. Put in the oven in the morning, and your meal is ready by dinnertime.

6 to 8 pounds of beef brisket, trimmed

½ cup ketchup

½ cup Worcestershire sauce

½ cup barbeque sauce

½ cup water

½ cup brown sugar

½ tsp. salt

¼ tsp. pepper

Preheat oven to 475°. Place brisket in a 9 x 13-inch pan and bake for 30 minutes uncovered. Meanwhile, combine remaining ingredients in sauce pan and mix well. Bring to a boil for 1 minute. Remove brisket from oven and pour sauce over meat and cover with foil. Reduce heat to 250° and bake for 5 to 6 hours. Slice thin and serve with your favorite BBQ sauce.

Serves 8 to 10.

Carne con Papas

Steak and potatoes cut into tender bite size pieces sautéed with onions and peppers. Cutting the meat and the vegetables in the same uniform size will make the dish not only appealing to the eye, but it actually tastes better. Serve this dish with warmed flour tortillas.

2 pounds top sirloin, cut into 1-inch cubes or smaller

1 Tbsp. salt

½ Tbsp. black pepper

½ Tbsp. granulated garlic

1 Tbsp. olive oil

1 medium onion, chopped

1 bell pepper, chopped

2 tomatoes, diced

2 medium potatoes, cut into 1-inch cubes or smaller (cut same size as meat)

½ cup tomato sauce

Place meat in a large skillet or stockpot over medium heat and season with salt, pepper and garlic. Cover and simmer until meat is just barely cooked through, about 5 to 8 minutes. Remove all juices and set aside. Add 1 tablespoon of oil to the meat and add onion, bell pepper, tomatoes and potatoes. Let cook until onion is slightly browned. Add tomato sauce and juices from meat and simmer over medium heat for about 15 minutes, stirring often.

Serve with warm flour tortillas.

Serves 4 to 6.

Classic Mexican Enchiladas — Torte Style

These authentic enchiladas are out-of-this-world delicious. Simple ingredients keep this one a classic. Thank you to the Gutierrez family for sharing their recipe.

1 cup enchilada sauce (recipe on following page)

20 corn tortillas

3 cups shredded mozzarella cheese

1 to 2 white onions, finely chopped

1 bunch fresh cilantro, chopped (optional)

1 lime, quartered (optional)

Canola oil, for frying

Heat enchilada sauce in a skillet or saucepan.

Put ½ inch to 1 inch of oil in a separate small saucepan or skillet and heat until very hot. Place one corn tortilla gently into hot oil (oil should be bubbly) and fry 5 to 8 seconds on each side. Remove tortilla from oil (using two forks gently so tortilla won't tear) and place tortilla into enchilada sauce; turn to coat both sides of tortilla with sauce. Place tortilla on serving plate. Top the tortilla with a small handful of mozzarella cheese and a few chopped onions. Repeat process, frying another tortilla, dipping it into sauce, place on top of first tortilla then cover the second layer with shredded mozzarella and chopped onions (amount of onions can be adjusted to taste). Repeat until you have five layers of tortillas. Top final layer with mozzarella cheese and fresh chopped cilantro.

Serve immediately with a wedge of lime.

Serves 4.

Enchilada Sauce

This batch makes enough sauce to freeze and save for another day.

25 to 35 dried New Mexico chilies* cleaned, seeds and stems removed

Salt

1 tsp. cumin

4 cloves garlic, halved

Water, about 4 cups

Thoroughly rinse cleaned chilies 2 to 3 times in a stock pot with cold water. Once rinsed cover chilies with enough water that most chilies are submerged. Place garlic into pot with chilies and water. Place pot on stove and bring to a boil. Once boiling reduce heat to simmer and partially cover pot with a lid. Simmer for 20 to 30 minutes then remove from heat.

Drain chilies and reserve liquid. Place chilies (including garlic) in a blender until half full. Add one to two cups of the reserved liquid to the chilies. Puree mixture in the blender for at least 2 minutes, being sure the chilies have been finely ground. Check mixture. If mixture is too thin, add another few chilies. If mixture is too thick add just a bit more liquid. Continue to puree.

Pour pureed mixture through a fine mesh strainer. This will remove any tiny bits of skin from the chilies. Help mixture through strainer with a spoon, slowly stirring to extract the liquid. Once all the liquid has been strained you will be left with a thick paste in your strainer. Throw the paste away. Your pot of gold is the liquid you've extracted. Repeat process with remaining chilies and reserved liquid until all of the chilies have been pureed. In some cases you may have reserve liquid left over. That is okay. You can use it if you need to thin the sauce, or if not, throw away.

At this point the sauce may be frozen for later use, or proceed as follows:

Place sauce in a large skillet. Add cumin. Bring to a low boil for 10 minutes or until thick (not too watery). Add salt to taste. Should your mixture be too thin add the following: 1 tablespoon cornstarch mixed with 3 tablespoons cold water. Add cornstarch mixture to sauce. Bring to low boil for 8 minutes.

Makes about 4 cups.

Dried New Mexico chilies can be found at most supermarkets or Latin-American grocers. I prefer the medium-hot chilies.

Mamasita's Burritos

This is delicious. Filled burritos baked in a casserole. Good for any night of the week.

1½ pounds lean ground beef

1 medium onion, chopped

½ tsp. cumin

½ tsp. garlic powder

Salt and pepper

2¼ cups salsa

12 to 20 tortillas (6- or 8-inch size)

16 oz. Monterey jack cheese, grated

Chopped lettuce

Chopped tomatoes

Sour cream

Chopped cilantro

Grease a 9 x 13-inch baking pan. Brown ground beef and onion in a skillet until onion is tender and beef brown. Drain off excess fat. Season with cumin, garlic, chili powder and salt and pepper to taste. Add salsa. Remove from heat and set aside. Fill each tortilla with a portion of the meat mixture and some monterey jack cheese and roll up. Place each burrito onto baking dish; lining them in a row as you make them.

SAUCE:

1 – 8 oz. can tomato sauce

¼ tsp. ground cumin

¼ tsp. chili powder

Combine sauce ingredients then spread over top of burritos in the pan. Add remaining cheese over top. Bake at 400° for 20 to 30 minutes. Lift each burrito gently out of baking dish onto a serving plate. Top with lettuce, tomatoes, cilantro and sour cream.

Makes 12 burritos. (Serves 6 to 8).

Taco Pie

Fun, easy to make and delicious

TACO MEAT FILLING:

1 pound lean ground beef

1½ cup onion, chopped

1 pkg. taco seasoning mix

¾ cup water

TOPPING:

1 cup shredded cheddar cheese

1 cup shredded lettuce

1 cup chopped tomatoes

TACO CRUST:

1½ to 2 cups all-purpose flour

1 package active dry yeast

1 Tbsp. sugar

2 tsp. finely chopped onion

¾ tsp. salt

⅔ cup warm water

2 Tbsp. oil

½ cup crushed tortilla corn chips

In medium mixing bowl, combine 1 cup flour, yeast, sugar, onion, and salt; mix well. Add very warm water and oil to flour mixture. Mix by hand until almost smooth. Stir in corn chips and enough remaining flour to make a stiff batter. Spread in well-greased 10-inch pie pan, forming a rim around edge. Cover; let rise in warm place about 20 minutes.

Brown ground beef and onions in a skillet. Add taco seasoning package and ¾ cup water. Simmer 20 minutes.

Spread meat filling over dough. Bake at 375° for 30 to 35 minutes until edge is crisp and light golden brown. Sprinkle cheese, lettuce and tomatoes on top. Serve immediately.

Serves 6 to 8.

Stuffed Cabbage

Delicious stuffed cabbage on a cool fall night. Try it with a side of mashed potatoes.

2 medium onions, minced

2 cloves garlic, minced

3 Tbsp. butter

3 pounds lean ground beef (may substitute 1½ pounds with lean ground pork)

1 Tbsp. paprika

2 tsp. salt

2 tsp. ground black pepper

¾ cup rice, washed and drained

1 large head fresh cabbage

1 pound sauerkraut, rinsed

1½ cups tomato juice

Lightly brown onions and garlic in butter. Cool slightly. Thoroughly mix onion-garlic mixture with ground beef, paprika, salt, pepper and rice; set aside.

Core cabbage and place in a pot. Pour boiling salted water over it and let it stand in the hot water for about 10 to 20 minutes, until the cabbage leaves are soft. Carefully separate leaves from head and cut hard core from each leaf.

Place 3 to 4 tablespoons of the meat mixture on each leaf and roll the leaf loosely, tucking in or pinching the ends closed. (The stuffing will expand during cooking, so if you roll the leaves too tightly, the rolls will burst.)

Shred the smaller leaves of cabbage. Shape any remaining meat mixture into meatballs. Place about half the sauerkraut across the bottom of an enamel or stainless-steel pot or roaster. Arrange the cabbage rolls on top of the sauerkraut along with any meatballs. Cover with the rest of the sauerkraut and any leftover shreds of fresh cabbage. Pour tomato juice over top.

Cover and cook in an electric roaster or place in a 275° oven for 1½ hours. Shake the pot occasionally to keep the bottom layer from burning. Serve immediately.

NOTE: *Flouring your hands will help in the stuffing and rolling process.*

Makes about 6 to 8 servings.

Bierocks

Great memories from the Schmidtberger's annual Octoberfest. I always stuffed a few of these yummies into my pocket for the ride home.

DOUGH:

2 cups lukewarm potato water*

5 Tbsp. sugar

1 Tbsp. salt

1 pkg. dry yeast

2 Tbsp. Crisco shortening

5 to 6 cups flour

In a medium bowl mix together 1¾ cups potato water with the sugar, salt and Crisco. In a separate bowl combine ¼ cup warm potato water with yeast and stir well. When yeast mixture begins to bubble (about 8 minutes) pour yeast mixture into potato mixture. Mix in 5 cups of flour with the yeast potato mixture (enough flour to handle dough easily). Knead dough. Add additional flour if necessary. Cover and let rise 1½ hours or until doubled in size (in a warm place, free of drafts).

Punch down and roll out dough. Cut into 4-inch squares; add filling and pinch closed. Cover and let rise ½ hour. Bake bierocks in a preheated 375° oven for 25 minutes or until nicely browned.

FILLING:

3 pounds lean ground beef

2 large onions, finely chopped

5 cups shredded cabbage (about 2 heads)

Salt and pepper

Brown ground meat in a large skillet or stock pot. Add onions and sauté or simmer on low heat until onions are cooked through. Add salt and pepper to taste. Add shredded cabbage and simmer ½ hour. Drain most of liquid off of meat mixture before filling dough.

*POTATO WATER: Add 1 medium peeled and diced potato to about 1¾ cups water. Bring to boil for approximately 6 to 8 minutes. Break up cooked potato in the water so that it becomes part of the liquid.

Makes approximately 20 to 25 bierocks.

NOTE: *To reheat bierocks, place them in the oven at 300° (or toaster oven) for about 10 to 12 minutes. For a crispier exterior, heat them uncovered.*

Chicken Kiev

This recipe was given to me by a friend of mine who is the executive chef and owner of the Candle Keller Restaurant in McMurray, Pennsylvania. A delicious, simple and exciting way to prepare chicken.

1 – 8 oz. package of cream cheese, room temperature

2 sticks of butter, room temperature

¼ tsp. garlic powder

1 tsp. fresh chives, minced

Salt and pepper

6 boneless, skinless chicken breast halves

1 cup cracker crumbs

1 tsp. dried rosemary

Combine cream cheese and butter in a bowl using a spatula. Add garlic powder, minced chives and pinch or two of salt and fresh cracked pepper. Stir to combine. Pour mixture onto a sheet of waxed paper. Using the waxed paper, form mixture into a log shape about 1 inch thick. Roll up and wrap with the waxed paper and place log into the freezer. After the cream cheese log has hardened, proceed with the following:

Pound chicken breast halves between two sheets of waxed paper. (If the chicken breast is very thick you can even cut each breast in half horizontally.) Remove cream cheese log from freezer (once it has hardened). Place the breast halves on a work surface. Cut about a 1 inch or so piece of the cream cheese mixture from the log and place onto the chicken breast. Roll up the chicken breast with the cream cheese and secure with a tooth pick. Repeat with remaining chicken breasts and cream cheese pieces.

Spray a baking dish with non-stick spray or rub surface with a pat of butter. Preheat oven to 350°. Place cracker crumbs into a bowl, season with salt and pepper. Roll each stuffed chicken breast in the cracker crumbs then place onto baking dish. Sprinkle tops of chicken with a few sprigs of rosemary. Place in oven and bake for 1 hour. Remove from oven, remove the toothpicks from the chicken, and serve. Great with roasted and mashed potatoes and tossed green salad.

Serves 4 to 6.

Parmesan Chicken

Not to be confused with Chicken Parmesan. This moist, delicious chicken recipe was given to me by my cousin Joanne Bier, who had prepared it for one of her parties I attended. I was amazed how simple and easy-to-prepare this fabulous meal was.

½ cup melted butter or margarine

2 tsp. Dijon mustard

1 tsp. Worcestershire Sauce

½ tsp. salt

1 cup dry bread crumbs, Italian style

½ to ¾ cup grated parmesan cheese

6 to 8 boneless, skinless chicken breasts, halves

In a shallow bowl or plate combine melted butter, mustard, Worcestershire sauce and salt. In a paper or plastic bag combine bread crumbs and parmesan cheese. Dip chicken in butter mixture, then shake in crumb mixture. Place in ungreased 9 x 13 x 2-inch pan. Drizzle with any remaining batter mixture.

Bake at 350° for about 1 hour or until chicken is no longer pink and juices are clear.

Makes 6 to 8 servings.

Chinese Chicken Satay

½ cup soy sauce

⅓ cup granulated sugar

1 tsp. salt

1 tsp. dried grated orange peel

1 clove garlic, minced

¼ tsp. black pepper

2 whole boneless, skinless chicken breasts cut into 1-inch strips

8-inch bamboo, wooden or metal skewers (if wooden, soak 30 minutes in water)

Combine first six ingredients in a small bowl, stirring until sugar dissolves. Transfer to large plastic resealable bag. Add chicken strips, seal bag and turn several times to coat chicken. Refrigerate at least 2 hours or overnight.

Preheat oven to 350°. Line baking pan with foil. Drain chicken and discard marinade. Thread chicken gently onto skewer. Set in baking pan. Bake until cooked through, about 45 to 50 minutes. Chicken can also be grilled over medium heat for about 8 to 12 minutes.

Serves 4.

Chicken and Wild Rice Casserole

Great recipe to make ahead and freeze. Good for unexpected guests, Sunday dinner or a potluck.

2 whole boneless skinless chicken breasts (4 halves)

4 cups water

1 cup sherry (or one additional cup of water)

1 medium onion, quartered

½ cup diced celery

½ tsp. curry powder

1 tsp. salt

1 pound fresh mushrooms

¼ cup margarine

2 – 6 oz. packages long grain wild rice with seasoning packets

1 – 10.5 oz. can cream of mushroom soup

1 cup sour cream

Put chicken breasts, water, sherry, onion, celery, curry powder and salt in medium pan. Cover and bring to boil. Reduce heat and simmer 30 to 40 minutes, or until cooked through. Remove chicken from broth; strain and reserve broth. When chicken is cool, chop coarsely. Reserve 10 small mushroom caps for decoration. Slice rest of mushrooms and sauté in margarine 5 minutes. Cook rice according to package directions (be sure to follow instructions for 2-box preparation), except substitute 1 cup of reserved chicken broth for 1 cup of the water.

Combine chicken, sautéed mushrooms and rice with soup and sour cream. Place mixture in large casserole or 9 x 13-inch baking dish. (At this point the casserole can be frozen or covered and refrigerated overnight. Allow to thaw before proceeding.)

Arrange mushroom caps in a circle on top of casserole and bake uncovered at 350° for 45 minutes or until lightly browned and bubbly. Parsley and lemon slices also make attractive garnishes.

Serves 8 to 10.

Diced Pork Sauce with Polenta

We were always delighted when our grandmother and aunties made polenta with pork for Sunday dinner. We have such great memories of sharing this and other delicious meals around the dinner table as we grew up in our Italian family.

4 to 5 boneless pork loin chops (1½ inches thick)

½ tsp. sage

1 cup onions, diced

½ tsp. marjoram

4 to 5 garlic cloves, minced

½ tsp. thyme

4 Tbsp. butter

½ tsp. rosemary

2 Tbsp. olive oil

¼ tsp. cayenne

1 Tbsp. sesame oil

4 to 5 bay leaves

1 cup diced tomatoes

¼ cup dry white wine

½ cup mushrooms, sliced and sautéed

48 oz. quality chicken stock

¾ cup browned flour*

¾ cup fresh parsley, chopped

Cut pork into ¾-inch cubes. Sauté onion in hot butter and oil about 10 minutes. Remove onion and set aside. Leave oil in pan. Add the diced meat and brown lightly about 20 minutes. Pan bottom will begin to pick up a little color. Add garlic and the cooked onions. Add chicken stock, bay leaves, sage, marjoram, thyme, rosemary, cayenne and tomatoes.

Bring to a simmer and continue cooking about one hour until meat is tender. Add browned flour, wine and mushrooms. Simmer ½ hour to blend flavors. Add handful of chopped parsley.

*BROWNED FLOUR: You can make this ahead. Keep in refrigerator. Place 1 cup flour in an 8-inch skillet at very low temperature. Keep mixing and heating until flour is dark beige. May take about 2 hours on low heat. Burns quickly and needs constant attention should you decide to use high heat. I've found that microwaving the flour in a shallow dish in 1- or 2-minute intervals, stirring between each interval, produces browned flour, as well.

POLENTA: My grandmother and her brothers would never have considered preparing polenta from a box, nor at that time was it available in a box. Since the early 1900s my grandmother Louise along with her sister, my Aunt Mary, would slowly add cornmeal to water and consistently stir the mixture for a good 45 minutes or more until it was thick and perfect. At that point the polenta would be poured onto a platter or board and sat for a few minutes until firm. Polenta was always cut with a string as to keep it in perfect form. Polenta is now available in most grocery stores in the grain, rice and pasta section. Today's boxed polenta is imported from Italy and can be prepared in minutes.

TO SERVE THIS DISH OLD-SCHOOL STYLE: Cut polenta into desired squares. Have each guest cut square in half horizontally. In the middle of the two polenta pieces we always placed a thick slice or two of brick cheese. Top polenta square with a ladle of the scrumptious diced pork.

TODAY'S POLENTA (This is my favorite way to prepare polenta): In a small bowl whisk together 1 cup yellow cornmeal and 1 cup water. In a medium saucepan, bring 3¼ cups water, 2 teaspoons salt and ⅛ teaspoon ground pepper to a rapid boil. Gradually stir in cornmeal mixture. Reduce heat to simmer, stirring frequently until mixture is thick, 5 to 8 minutes. Remove from heat. Stir in 1 cup grated fontina cheese and 2 tablespoons butter until melted.

Ladle a scoop of creamy polenta into a bowl. Top polenta with a ladle of diced pork.

Excellent and typical side dishes would be sautéed green beans and mushrooms.

Serves 8.

Lettiann's Italian Meatballs

These are tender and delicious. I like to make these meatballs larger for a more dramatic effect. I bake them in the oven and then drop them into Lettiann's Sunday Sauce to finish cooking.

1½ pounds quality ground beef *

2 eggs, beaten

½ tsp. salt

¼ tsp. black pepper

¼ cup onion, finely chopped

3 Tbsp. grated parmesan cheese

½ cup plain cracker crumbs

1 Tbsp. water

In a large bowl combine all ingredients gently. The more you work the meatball mixture, the less tender they will turn out once they are cooked. Gently form into 1½- to 2-inch diameter meatballs. Place on a metal baking sheet that has been covered with parchment paper. Bake in a preheated 350° oven for 15 minutes. Remove from oven and gently drop into your stock pot of Italian tomato sauce. Here the meatballs will absorb the flavors of the sauce while they finish cooking. They can be left in the sauce for as long as you'd like. They will not overcook.

I use organic 85% ground beef. I would caution against using anything leaner as the meatballs will likely be less tender and you could sacrifice flavor when using a leaner cut of meat.

Makes approximately 16 to 18 meatballs.

Mustard-Bourbon Kebabs

1 pound boneless pork chops ¾-inch thick, cut into 1-inch cubes

4 Tbsp. Dijon-style mustard

4 Tbsp. brown sugar

2 Tbsp. bourbon

2 Tbsp. soy sauce

In a self-sealing plastic bag, combine all ingredients and mix well. Refrigerate overnight. Remove pork from marinade. Thread pork onto skewers (if using wooden skewers soak them in water at least 30 minutes before using to prevent them from burning). Broil or grill kebabs about 4 inches from heat source, turning occasionally, for 8 to 10 minutes, until nicely browned.

Serve with hot rice and a tossed salad.

Makes 4 servings.

Pork Chili Stew

Prepare this dish ahead of time and it tastes even better the next day. It also freezes well. So nice to have this on hand for a tailgate party or a Sunday afternoon of football. Serve with warmed flour tortillas.

2 to 3 pounds boneless pork shoulder, room temperature

1 onion, diced

4 cloves garlic, minced

1 Tbsp. crushed dried hot red peppers (to taste)

2½ tsp. ground cumin

2½ tsp. ground coriander

4 tsp. chili powder

¾ tsp. dried oregano

¾ tsp. dried marjoram

½ tsp. cayenne pepper

2 cups lightly-crushed canned tomatoes (not plum) with their juices

3 cups basic chicken stock

2 – 19 oz. cans kidney beans, drained and rinsed

Salt to taste

In a stock pot brown pork on all sides over high heat. Remove pork and set aside. Stir in onion, garlic, spices, and herbs. Lower heat and cook 2 minutes.

Return meat to pot. Stir in tomatoes and chicken stock. Bring to boil. Lower heat and simmer, covered, for 2 hours and 15 minutes. Turn meat every 30 minutes. Remove heat from soup and allow to cool slightly. Skim as much fat from top of soup as possible. Slice meat across the grain into thin slices.

Return meat to pot. Add beans and salt and heat through. Serve over white rice topped with shredded cheddar cheese and sour cream.

Serves 8 to 10.

Baked Ham'ich

Individual hot sandwiches wrapped in foil. Interestingly good. Great for a casual luncheon, shower or tailgate party.

1 pound good-quality baked ham, chipped and shaved

½ pound grated sharp cheddar cheese

3 hard boiled eggs, chopped

⅓ cup sweet relish

⅓ cup bottled chili sauce

¼ cup onions, chopped (or to taste)

½ cup mayonnaise

12 hotdog buns from the bakery

Stir in a bowl all ingredients except buns. Chill overnight. Slice buns in half and fill each with a portion of the mixture. Wrap separately in foil. Bake in oven 350° for 20 minutes, or place the foil-wrapped sandwiches on a grill over indirect low-to-medium heat. Close the lid until warm, about 15 minutes.

Makes 12 sandwiches.

Dryaniki (Filled Potato Pancakes)

This recipe is from Galina Ross, one of my team members who was born and raised in Belarus. Her home town is known for potatoes and they used them in almost everything. This potato dish is one of her favorites as it brings back so many wonderful childhood memories of cold snowy winters standing by the stove with her mom, preparing this delicious dish.

5 to 6 medium potatoes

2 Tbsp. flour

salt to taste

FILLING:

½ lb. ground turkey, chicken, beef or pork

½ of a medium onion, minced.

1 to 2 garlic cloves, minced

Salt and black pepper to taste

Chopped parsley to taste

Grate potatoes on the finest grater, stir in salt and flour.

Brown the meat in a skillet along with salt/pepper, onion and garlic.

Add oil to a separate skillet. Once the pan is hot, spoon one or two tablespoons of the potato mixture into the heated skillet and add a little bit (¼ to ½ teaspoon) of the meat filling over the potato mixture, then spoon a tablespoon or two of the potato mixture on top. Cook for a few minutes then flip it and cook it on the other side for a few minutes.

Serve it with sour cream and chopped scallions (optional).

Note: Galina's mom did not cook the meat filling in advance; however, you may, if you'd like.

Makes approximately 6 potato cakes.

SWEETS

Butterscotch Bavarian Cream Pie

My Aunt Letty was the dietitian for a very popular department store restaurant. The department store was Kaufmann's in Pittsburgh and the restaurant name was Tic Toc. I remember dressing up and going to the Santa Luncheon they had there every year when I was a little girl. It was so fun to visit my Aunt Letty at work. I believe that is when I had my first glimpse of a commercial kitchen. Tic Toc is likely where my "foodie" passion began.

9-inch pie shell, baked

1 cup whipping cream

1 envelope unflavored gelatin

¼ cup cold water

½ pound caramels

½ cup hot water

¼ tsp. salt

½ tsp. vanilla extract

Whip the whipping cream with a rotary beater or mixer until peaks form; then set in refrigerator until needed. Soften gelatin in cold water, set aside.

Melt caramels in hot water, over low heat, until a smooth sauce is formed. Stir in softened gelatin and salt and stir until gelatin is dissolved. Cool to room temperature. Fold in whipped cream and vanilla. Gently ladle into pie crust and refrigerate until firm.

Serve with additional whipped cream.

Serves 6-8.

Famous Fudge

Years ago a coworker would bring this fudge into the office every Christmas season. Though I'm usually not a big fan of fudge, this recipe is one that I now make every year, too.

2 Tbsp. butter or margarine

⅔ cup undiluted evaporated milk

1½ cup granulated sugar

¼ tsp. salt

2 cups mini-marshmallows

1½ cups semi-sweet chocolate chips

1 tsp. vanilla extract

½ cup chopped pecans or walnuts

Butter an 8-inch square pan. In a medium saucepan combine butter, evaporated milk, sugar and salt. Bring to a boil over medium heat, stirring constantly. Boil 4 to 6 minutes, still stirring constantly. Remove from heat and immediately stir in marshmallows, chocolate chips, vanilla and nuts.

Stir vigorously for 1 minute or until marshmallows melt and blend. Pour into pan. Cool and cut into squares.

Fruit Pizza

Perfect dessert during the hot days of summer when the freshest of berries are available. This dessert is also a show stopper. It is very colorful and impressive.

1 pkg. Pillsbury sugar cookie dough (in refrigerator section of grocery store)

8 oz. cream cheese

½ cup sugar

1 tsp. vanilla

Your choice of fresh fruit: raspberries, blueberries, strawberries, kiwi, etc.

SAUCE:

⅜ cup water

⅛ cup orange juice

⅛ cup lemon juice

1½ tsp. cornstarch

Dash of salt

½ cup sugar (optional)

Line tart pan with cookie dough. Bake 20 minutes, and allow to cool.

Mix cream cheese, ½ cup sugar and 1 teaspoon vanilla until creamy. Spread mixture on dough.

Layer fruit, using your artistic ability.

NOTE: Topping the fruit pizza with this sauce is optional. I only make it if time permits. It is delicious without it as well.

In a sauce pan mix the water, orange juice, lemon juice, corn starch, a dash of salt and optional sugar. Bring to a boil, cook 1 minute; cool. Use sauce to glaze fruit.

Chill thoroughly.

Serves about 8.

Spicy Almond Biscotti

My Dad's favorite. Every winter his cousin Loretta would send him these biscotti from Boston.

1 cup granulated sugar

1 cup dark brown sugar

2 eggs

2 tsp. cinnamon

½ tsp. ground cloves

2 tsp. baking powder

⅓ cup oil

4 Tbsp. water

2 cup whole almonds (not blanched)

2½ cups flour

Do not use an electric mixer. Use wooden spoon. Mix first 8 ingredients. Add flour and almonds. Mix. Separate dough into fourths. Form each into a loaf.

Place 2 loaves on each cookie sheet. Brush top with egg yolk and 1 teaspoon milk. Bake 20 minutes at 375°. Remove from oven and let cool slightly. Cut into slices on the diagonal before they get cold. Lay them cut side up on the cookie sheet and return to oven for 15 minutes at 325°. Cool on racks.

Makes about 40 biscotti.

Chocolate–Pecan Biscotti

3 eggs

1 cup sugar

¼ tsp. oil

1 tsp. vanilla extract

2½ cups of flour

2 Tbsp. unsweetened cocoa powder

1 tsp. baking soda

Pinch of salt

1 cup mini semi-sweet chocolate chips

1 cup pecan halves

Set the oven at 350°. Rub a baking sheet with oil or line it with parchment paper. In the bowl of an electric mixer, beat the eggs, sugar, oil and vanilla for 2 minutes. With the mixer set on its lowest speed, mix in the flour, cocoa, baking soda and salt. Mix in the chocolate chips and the nuts just until the nuts break up slightly.

Spoon the dough on to the prepared baking sheets in two strips, making sure there is plenty of room between them. Flatten and smooth the logs with a metal spatula so they are 12 inches long and about 4 inches wide. Bake for 40 minutes or until they are golden brown. Remove from oven and let set for 5 minutes (at this point you may slide logs onto a board if you choose), then using a sharp serrated knife cut the strips on the diagonal into ½-inch slices. Place the slices cut-side-up on the baking sheet. Return the sheet to the oven and bake the slices for 15 to 20 minutes. Remove them from the oven and transfer them to a rack. Store cooled cookies in an airtight container.

Makes about 24 biscotti.

Oatmeal Peanut Butter Cookies

Our family is from western Pennsylvania. There is a large Amish population in the middle and eastern part of our state. Somewhere along the way I was given this Amish cookie recipe.

1 cup sugar

1 cup brown sugar

1 cup shortening

1 cup peanut butter

3 eggs

1½ cups flour

1 tsp. baking soda

1 tsp. salt

1 tsp. vanilla

2 cups quick oats

1 cup chocolate morsels or raisins

Cream sugars and shortening. Add eggs and peanut butter. Beat well. Gradually add flour, salt and soda. Add vanilla. Stir in oats and chocolate chips or raisins.

Drop by heaping teaspoonful onto cookie sheet. Bake at 350° for 15 minutes.

Makes about 5 dozen.

Sugar Cookies

Cut out shapes of any kind with this great sugar cookie recipe. We enjoyed these cookies just as they are, not iced or decorated. Please eat and decorate them however you choose.

3 cups all-purpose flour

1 tsp. baking powder

¼ tsp. salt

1¼ cup granulated sugar

1 cup shortening

3 eggs

1 tsp. vanilla

Sift the flour, baking powder, salt and sugar in a large bowl. Add the shortening; cut the shortening into dry mix with a pastry blender or two forks. Cut in until evenly blended.

Add the eggs and vanilla and mix with the spoon. May need to use your hands. Sprinkle flour over pastry board. Make a ball of dough and roll out with floured rolling pin.

Use cookie cutters—hearts, animals, angels, etc. and cut out shapes. Bake quickly, about 12 minutes, in a 350° oven.

Makes about 7 dozen.

Raisin–Filled Cookies

This recipe is a sleeper. Fun to make and absolutely fabulous to eat. Great with a hot cup of tea.

FILLING:

¾ cup sugar

1 cup water

1 pound box raisins, ground*

1 Tbsp. lemon juice

Over medium heat bring to boil the filling ingredients, adding the lemon juice last. Remove from heat and cover.

Grind the raisins in a grinder or food processor. It actually makes the filling taste better. We used an old-fashioned hand-operated meat grinder.

COOKIE DOUGH:

1 cup brown sugar, packed

1 cup granulated sugar

1 cup shortening

2 eggs

1 tsp. vanilla

⅓ cup milk

4 cups flour

Pinch of salt

2 tsp. baking powder

Cream together sugars and shortening. Add eggs one at a time. Add milk and vanilla. In a separated bowl combine dry ingredients (flour, salt, baking powder). Gently add flour mixture, one cup at a time, to creamed sugar, Mix until smooth. Chill dough for one hour.

Generously grease cookie sheets then refrigerate them. Roll out dough on floured board. Cut dough into approximately 3-inch circles. (Can use top of a wine glass or similar). Place 1 teaspoon filling in the center of a dough circle then cover with another dough circle. Pinch or press side to close. Lots of filling makes a better cookie. Bake 8 to 10 minutes in a preheated 350° oven until golden brown. Watch carefully so they do not burn. Quickly sprinkle each cookie with granulated sugar after you remove it from the oven. Cool on wire racks.

Makes approximately 20 cookies.

Peanut Brittle

I like to wrap pieces of the peanut brittle in decorative food-safe bags and give to my co-workers right after Thanksgiving. During the holidays, I feel it is better to give gifts of food early in December, as the middle and latter parts of December can be hectic. This allows the recipient to enjoy your treat as well as giving you more time to relax and enjoy the holidays.

3 cups raw shelled peanuts

1½ tsp. baking soda

½ tsp. salt

2 cups sugar

1 cup light corn syrup

½ cup water

¼ cup unsalted butter

Preheat oven to 350°. Spread the peanuts in a 10 x 15-inch baking pan.*

Bake for 15 minutes. Transfer to bowl and keep warm.

Combine the baking soda and salt and set aside. Combine the sugar, corn syrup and water in a saucepan. Heat to boiling; boil rapidly until the syrup begins to turn golden, 275° on a candy thermometer. Add the nuts and continue to cook, stirring frequently, until the syrup is a clear, gold color, 295°. Remove from the heat and quickly stir in the butter and the baking soda mixture. Immediately pour into a heat-proof service such as a marble slab or metal sheet pan covered with parchment paper.

Let cool for 2 hours before breaking into pieces.

Makes about 2¼ pounds.

I use a ½-inch metal sheet pan and feel it works best.

Pizzelles

Pizzelles are an anise-flavored wafer Italian cookie which is made with a pizzelle iron. During Christmastime it was always funny that everyone in our family was giving each other pizzelles. Some were softer than others; some were crisp; some were brown; some remained a consistent creamy color. I still recall my aunts and grandmother discussing the difference between each of the stacks of pizzelles they received. I never imagined how they could find so much to discuss about this simple cookie. After trying many different variations of pizzelle dough over the years, this one has remained my constant favorite.

12 eggs

3¾ cup sugar

7 cups flour

1 Tbsp. anise oil

2 Tbsp. lemon extract

2 Tbsp. vanilla extract

¼ tsp. cinnamon

2 cups margarine, softened

Beats eggs well. Add sugar gradually, continuing to beat in mixer. Add margarine, flavorings and beat until smooth. Add flour a little at a time, mix well. Chill dough 2 hours or overnight to blend flavors.

Place 1½ teaspoons or so of dough onto center grate of pizzelle iron and close lid. Be sure mixture doesn't come out the side of iron. If it does, use less next time. Hold iron closed for 30 seconds or so. When pizzelle is slightly brown remove from the iron and place on wire rack. Let cool and crisp up.

Makes 4 dozen.

Gallette

A Belgian cookie my Aunt Letty would make in abundance only once a year.

1 pound butter softened

1 pound sugar (2 cups)

1 cup light brown sugar

2 Tbsp. vanilla

1 pound eggs (8 or 9), separated

1 pound flour (4 cups before sifting)

Beat egg whites until stiff. Set aside. Begin next step in a clean mix bowl. Cream butter with the white and brown sugars. Cream well. Add the vanilla. Add the egg yolks and cream well.

On low speed blend in the sifted flour a little at a time. Fold in the egg white. With a waffle iron (one which has 4 squares) set on medium heat, spoon approximately ¼ cup of batter into 8 spots on your waffle iron. Cookies should be about 2½ inches in diameter. Bake until golden brown, usually about 2 minutes.

Use a little fork to gently lift the cookie from the waffle iron grid. Place cookie on a rack where it will firm up as it cools.

Makes about 165 small cookies.

My aunts would neatly wrap 3 cookies in waxed paper, with a small square piece of waxed paper tucked in between each cookie. I would imagine the cutting of more than 300 small squares of waxed paper would be more time-consuming than the cookie making.

Nana's Sour Cream Coffee Cake

Great for weekend guests.

NUT FILLING AND TOPPING:

⅓ cup brown sugar

1 cup pecans or walnuts

1 tsp. cinnamon

¼ cup granulated sugar

4 Tbsp. unsalted butter

Pinch of salt

BATTER:

1 cup granulated sugar

½ cup unsalted butter

2 eggs

2 cups sifted flour

1 tsp. baking soda

1 tsp. baking powder

¼ tsp. salt

1 cup sour cream

1 tsp. vanilla

FOR FILLING AND TOPPING:
Combine all ingredients together. Set aside.

FOR BATTER: Cream together butter and sugar. Beat in eggs one at a time. Continue beating approximately one minute until light and fluffy. Sift dry ingredients together. Mix sour cream and vanilla. Add to batter in 3 intervals, beginning and ending with dry ingredients, alternating with sour cream-vanilla mixture.

TO ASSEMBLE CAKE: Spread ½ of batter in bottom of buttered and floured 8- or 9-inch spring form pan. Top with ½ of nut mixture. Spread remaining batter over nut filling, top with remaining nut topping. Bake at 375° for 35 to 40 minutes. When done toothpick comes out clean.

Serves about 8.

Birthday Cake

Due to the expense of raising five children in Russia, Galina's parents could not afford store-bought birthday cakes or parties. On the eve of each birthday her mom would bake this beautiful cake. The aroma would fill the house. She recalls it being one of the most exciting of times. Each time she makes this cake it brings back those loving, special memories.

1¾ cups all-purpose flour

¾ cup dark cocoa powder

2 cups sugar

1½ tsp. baking powder

1½ tsp. baking soda

1 tsp. salt

2 eggs

1 cup milk

½ cup vegetable oil

2 tsp. vanilla extract

1 cup boiling water

CREAM:

16 oz. mascarpone

24 oz. sour cream

2 cups sugar

4 oz. cream cheese

Heat oven to 350°.

Grease, line and flour two 8-inch round baking pans.

Whisk together flour, cocoa, sugar, baking powder, baking soda and salt in a large bowl. To that add eggs, milk, oil, vanilla; mix it all together. Add the boiling water to the batter and stir well (batter will be thin). Pour batter into prepared pans.

Bake 40 to 45 min or until wooden skewer inserted in the center comes out clean.

Cool for 10 min; remove from the pans to wire racks. Cool completely before assembling the cake.

CREAM: Melt cream cheese a little bit in a microwave. Mix it with sour cream and sugar and beat on medium/high speed of a mixer for 2 minutes. Then add mascarpone and chill the cream a little bit before assembling the cake. You can decorate it in any way you want. I usually melt some chocolate and pour it on top of the cake.

Serves 8-10.

Pecan Balls

Surprise your guest with this cool, impressive treat. Very popular dessert in Pennsylvania—it is on the menu at many restaurants. This version is from the Tic Toc restaurant located in Kaufmann's department store in Pittsburgh where my Aunt Letty worked.

1 gallon (+/-) Vanilla or Chocolate Ice Cream

2 cups pecans, chopped fine (not ground)

Butterscotch sauce* (recipe on following page)

Chocolate Sauce

Cover an empty 9 x 13-inch baking dish with plastic wrap. With a good size ice cream scooper, scoop out a ball of ice cream. Then roll the ice cream ball firmly into the chopped pecans to coat entire surface of the ice cream. As you finish each ball, place them on top of the plastic wrap and put into the freezer to harden. Placing the ice cream balls on the plastic wrap allows them to keep their shape.

When you are ready to serve the pecan balls, take an individual serving plate and drizzle it with butterscotch sauce and/or chocolate sauce, remove pecan ball from freezer and place one pecan ball on top of the plate, then drizzle generously with more butterscotch and/or chocolate sauce. Serve immediately.

Servings vary—you can make as many or as few pecan balls as you'd like.

Sauce can be made a day or two ahead.

K's Butterscotch Sauce

Great for Pecan Balls or as a topping for ice cream. From the Tic Toc restaurant located in Kaufmann's department store in Pittsburgh where my Aunt Letty worked.

15 oz. granulated sugar

½ cup Karo syrup light

2 cups (18%) coffee cream

1 cup half & half light cream

Mix ingredients in heavy sauce pan. Cook over medium-to-low heat, stirring until sugar dissolves. It needs to be watched carefully after it begins to boil. Stir down as it begins to bubble up. It will bubble up as it gets nearly finished, about 2 hours cooking time after it begins to boil. Cook until "double drop" collects when the spoon is held on edge above the sauce pan. Stir frequently as it cooks.

Remove from heat and pour into heat proof containers. Cool completely. Cover and refrigerate.

Makes about 2 cups.

Tiramisu

What a treat this delicious "pick me up" dessert is. This is the real deal.

1 large package of savoiardi (Italian ladyfinger cookies)

1½ cups strong espresso (mix 1½ cups water with 6 Tbsp. instant espresso powder)

½ cup Grand Marnier

17.5 oz. container of mascarpone cheese

5 Tbsp. dark rum

5 large egg yolks

2 Tbsp. sugar

1 pint whipping cream

1 tsp. vanilla

5 large egg whites

⅛ tsp. salt

3 Tbsp. sugar

1 small package blanched almonds sliced

2 Tbsp. unsweetened cocoa powder (preferably Dutch-process)

Select two round casserole Pyrex type dishes (2 quart capacity) or a 9 x 13 x 2½-inch pan. Line the bottom and sides with the savoiardi, saving some for the center. You need to cut them in half for the sides. Prepare the strong espresso and after it has cooled add ½ cup Grand Marnier. Use this mixture for dipping and moistening. Quickly dip each of the savoiardi from the casseroles and return to the casseroles. Set aside for later use.

Mix container of mascarpone cheese and the dark rum; blend until incorporated. Set aside. In the top of a double boiler over very low heat beat 5 egg yolks with 3 tablespoons sugar about 3 minutes until light. Remove from heat and quickly add this to the mascarpone mixture. Set aside.

Beat 1 pint whipping cream and 1 teaspoon vanilla extract until the cream just holds a firm shape. Fold part of the mascarpone mixture into the whipped cream then fold the whipped cream into the remaining mascarpone mixture. Set aside.

Using clean beaters, beat 5 egg whites and ⅛ teaspoon salt until they hold a soft shape. Gradually add 3 tablespoons sugar and continue to beat on high until whites hold a firm shape but not dry. Add the beaten whites all at once to the mascarpone and cream mixture and fold together. It takes patience to carefully fold over and over again until all whites are folded in. Pour a fourth of the mixture into each of the casseroles over the savoiardi. Dip more savoiardi to place a layer in center. Push into mixture and then cover with the remaining mascarpone mixture. Refrigerate.

Toast package of sliced blanched almonds, and when cool, place in a processor for a few minutes to chop fine. Sprinkle over the top of each casserole. Sift a layer of unsweetened cocoa over the top.

Clean rims and cover with plastic wrap. Continue to refrigerate overnight.

Serves 12 to 16 people.

Rum Cake

Be careful. Your nose may turn a bit red after a piece or two of this intoxicating cake.

CAKE:

1 cup chopped pecans or walnuts

1 – 18½ oz pkg. yellow cake mix

1 – 3¾ oz pkg. JELL-O Vanilla Instant Pudding and Pie Filling

4 eggs

½ cup cold water

½ cup vegetable oil

½ cup Bacardi dark rum (80 proof)

GLAZE:

¼ lb. butter

¼ cup water

1 cup granulated sugar

½ cup Bacardi dark rum (80 proof)

Preheat oven to 325°. Grease and flour 12-inch bundt pan. Sprinkle nuts over bottom of pan. Mix all cake ingredients together. Pour batter over nuts. Bake 1 hour. Cool.

GLAZE: Melt butter in saucepan. Stir in water and sugar. Boil 5 minutes, stirring constantly. Remove from heat. Stir in rum.

Invert on serving plate. Prick top. Spoon and brush glaze evenly over top and sides. Allow cake to absorb glaze. Repeat till glaze is used up.

Recipe courtesy of Bacardi Rum.

Serves about 8.

Nut Rolls

Another holiday staple. Nut rolls served cold, warm or at room temperature. Cut them as you eat them and spread with real butter. Delicious. My brother Eric would inhale these. These also make a great hostess gift.

DOUGH:

8 cups flour

¾ cup sugar

1 tsp. salt

1 pound margarine

1 cake yeast (small single size)

1 cup milk

4 eggs beaten

1 tsp. vanilla

NUT FILLING:

6 cups walnuts, chopped

2 cups milk

1 cup sugar

1 cup honey

1½ tsp. vanilla

Sift flour, sugar, salt. Cut in margarine to pea size. Dissolve yeast in warm milk and add beaten eggs and vanilla to mixture. Add to flour mix and knead until it comes clean with the fingers. Place in a large bowl, cover with tea towel and place in refrigerator overnight. When ready to bake, let dough stand at room temperature until soft. Separate into 4 portions. Roll one portion at a time on floured surface. Roll it thin.

Mix together filling ingredients and bring to a boil. Take off heat, let cool. Spread nut filling over all the dough surface. Roll loosely like jelly roll. Brush top with beaten egg and bake 45 minutes at 375° on a cookie sheet. Cool completely.

Wrap in butcher paper or plastic wrap. Tie with a pretty bow for a hostess gift.

Makes 4 loaves.

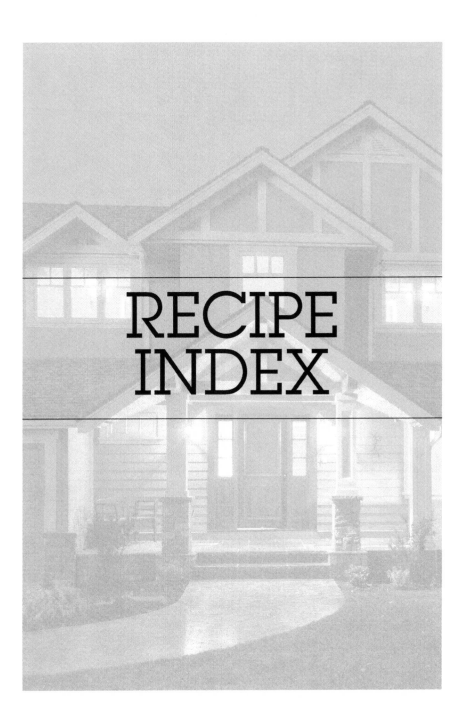

RECIPE INDEX

RECIPE INDEX

Acknowledgements

I wish to personally thank my dear family and friends for their recipe contributions, their inspiration and knowledge in creating this book.

About the Author

Lettiann Southerland is the owner of Lettiann & Associates Real Estate Services, LLC. Licensed in both Kansas and Missouri, Lettiann is a full time real estate agent with an emphasis on service, sales and marketing, and negotiating. As a result of her hard work and efforts, Lettiann has received the President's Club Award for her sales achievements for the past three years. She is a member of the Kansas City Regional Association of Realtors, the National Association of Realtors, the Missouri Real Estate Commission, and the Kansas Real Estate Commission. She has completed the Karrass Effective Negotiating Course.

Being an entrepreneur at heart, Lettiann has started and run various businesses and endeavors including: My Bella Zia, LLC, personal assistant services; Lettiann's Kitchen, catering services; and Toxic Secret Blog, a blog to bring awareness of the harmful effects pornography and related topics have on society today. She and her husband also own and manage several rental properties.

Lettiann has a passion for life. She is a self-proclaimed foodie, animal enthusiast, wine aficionado, vigilante, and crusader. In her spare time she enjoys cooking, yoga, snow skiing, and traveling. Her passions include family, healthy living, food and nutrition, supporting locally-owned businesses, and supporting the fight against human trafficking.

She currently resides with her family in Overland Park, Kansas. Lettiann can be reached at Lettiann@Lettiann.com or at 816-898-5477. Visit her on the web at www.Lettiann.com and www.HomesThatCook.com.

Space for your own recipes

_____

_____

_____

_____

_____

_____

_____

_____

_____

_____

_____

_____

_____

_____

_____

_____

_____

_____

_____

_____

_____

38810133R00099

Made in the USA
Middletown, DE
16 March 2019